SUPERSTARS!

CRUSH!

SCREEN
ACTORS
GUILD
AWARDS

SUPERSTARS!

CRUSH!

PRODUCED BY

President Susan Knopf
Writer Debra Mostow Zakarin
Editorial Assistant Chelsea M. Burris
Book designed by Annemarie Redmond/Annemarie Redmond Design, Inc.
Special thanks Andrij Borys/Andrij Borys Associates,
Michael Centore, Laura Ross

Publisher Jim Childs
Vice President, Finance Vandana Patel
Executive Director, Business Development Suzanne Albert
Executive Director, Marketing Services Carol Pittard
Executive Director, Marketing Susan Hettleman
Publishing Director Megan Pearlman
Associate Director of Publicity Courtney Greenhalgh
Assistant General Counsel Simone Procas
Assistant Director, Special Sales Ilene Schreider
Senior Marketing Manager, Sales Marketing Danielle Costa
Senior Manager, Business Development + Partnerships
Nina Fleishman Reed
Senior Production Manager Susan Chodakiewicz
Editor, Children's Books Jonathan White
Associate Prepress Manager Alex Voznesenskiy
Assistant Project Manager Hillary Hirsch
Assistant Production Manager Matthew Ryan

Editorial Director Stephen Koepp
Senior Editor Roe D'Angelo
Copy Chief Rina Bander
Design Manager Anne-Michelle Gallero
Editorial Operations Gina Scauzillo

SPECIAL THANKS TO Katherine Barnet, Brad Beatson, Jeremy Biloon, Rose Cirrincione, Assu Etsubneh, Mariana Evans, Christine Font, David Kahn, Jean Kennedy, Amy Mangus, Kimberly Marshall, Courtney Mifsud, Nina Mistry, Dave Rozzelle, Ricardo Santiago, Divyam Shrivastava, Holly Smith, Adriana Tierno

Published by Time Home Entertainment Inc.
1271 Avenue of the Americas, 6th floor • New York, NY 10020

ISBN 10: 1-61893-382-5
ISBN 13: 978-1-61893-382-9

We welcome your comments and suggestions about Time Home Entertainment Books. Please write to us at: Time Home Entertainment Books, Attention: Book Editors, P.O. Box 11016, Des Moines, IA 50336-1016. If you would like to order any of our hardcover Collector's Edition books, please call us at 1-800-327-6388, Monday through Friday, 7 a.m.–8 p.m., or Saturday, 7 a.m.–6 p.m., Central Time.

1 QGC 14

TABLE OF CONTENTS

ONE DIRECTION

The guys of One Direction may have finished third on Britain's *The X Factor* in 2010, but ever since then they have been topping the charts. With megahits "What Makes You Beautiful," "Live While We're Young," and "Story of My Life," 1D became the first band in U.S. Billboard 200 history to have their first three albums debut at number one.

Harry, Louis, Niall, Zayn, and Liam were all solo contestants on Britain's *The X Factor* in 2010. During an early round, rather than send them through or send them home, Simon Cowell decided to put them together to compete as a group. We're glad he did!

Didja know?

The lads may have more than 29 million facebook fans, but they don't take their success for granted. "We're as surprised by it as everyone else is," Zayn said. "We're living the dream," Niall added. (*60 Minutes Australia*)

The guys give it their all for their devoted Directioners during an appearance on *Good Morning America*.

HARRY STYLES

Harry Styles skyrocketed to superstardom overnight as the lead singer of One Direction. Whether performing on stage, meeting the fans, or hanging out with the lads, Harry is having a lot of fun.

IN THE KNOW

Full name: **Harry Edward Styles**
Nickname: **Hazza**
Birth date: **February 1, 1994**
Hometown: **Worcestershire, England**
Zodiac sign: **Aquarius**

KEEPIN' IT REAL

"I've got good friends around me, good family. I think I've got my head screwed on," Harry told **The Sun.**

LOSING HIS SHIRT

Harry supports a good cause. He donated his favorite shirt, the one he wore at London's Fashion Week, to charity in order to help raise money and awareness for UNICEF (the United Nations Children's Fund, the world's leading advocate for children).

LUCKY FANS

Connecting with the fans is totally on Harry's radar. He loves meeting them and they sure know how to show their appreciation.

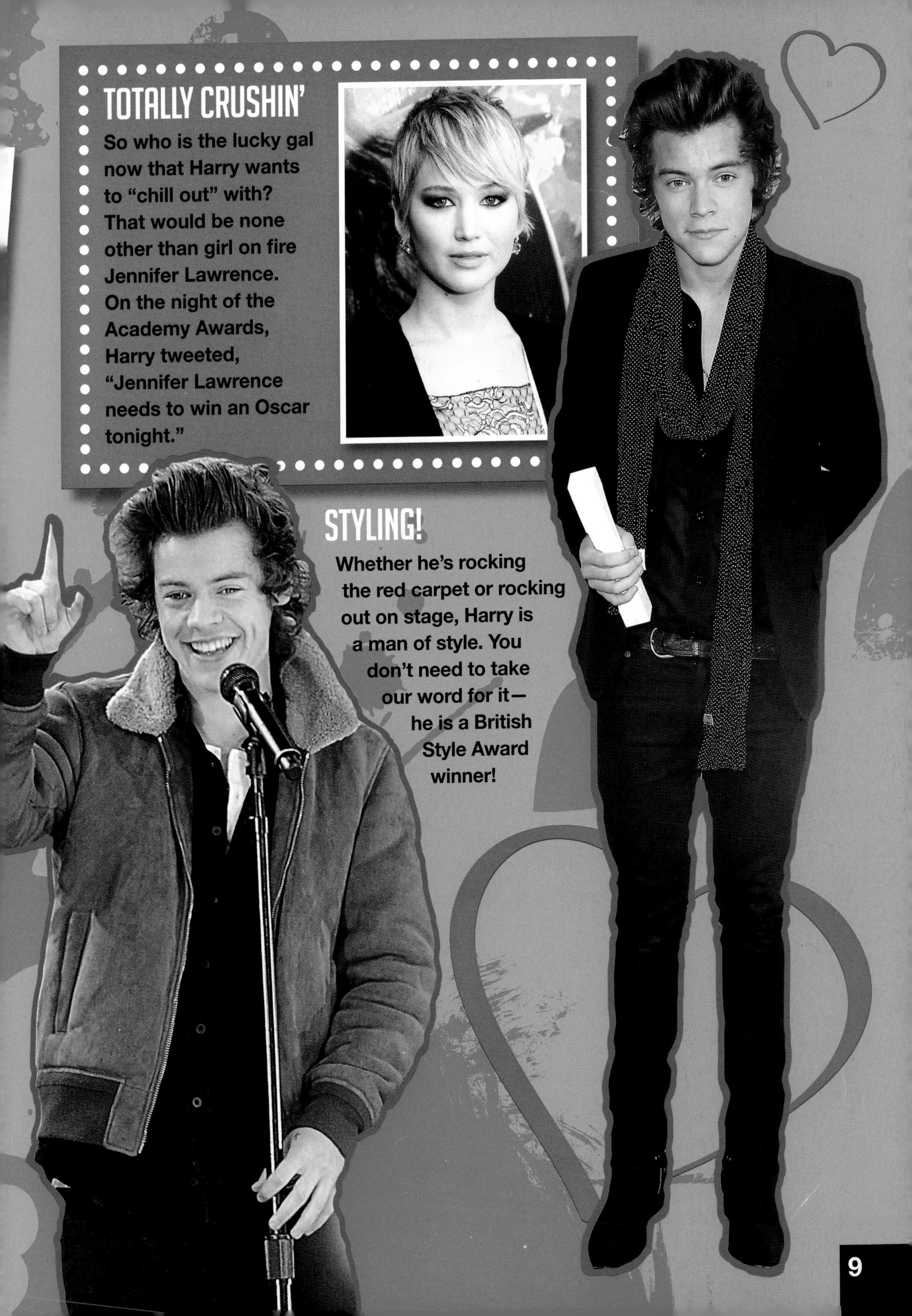

TOTALLY CRUSHIN'

So who is the lucky gal now that Harry wants to "chill out" with? That would be none other than girl on fire Jennifer Lawrence. On the night of the Academy Awards, Harry tweeted, "Jennifer Lawrence needs to win an Oscar tonight."

STYLING!

Whether he's rocking the red carpet or rocking out on stage, Harry is a man of style. You don't need to take our word for it— he is a British Style Award winner!

LOUIS TOMLINSON

Before Louis was part of One Direction, he was an actor in England. Following his younger twin sisters into acting, he played an extra in *Fat Friends* when he was eleven years old. He also had small roles in *If I Had You* and *Waterloo Road*. Louis is known as the prankster of 1D, and is always up for playing a good joke on one of his band mates. Once, he punked Harry by changing his name on Harry's cell phone to "Frankie Sanford," then called him repeatedly so that Harry had two dozen missed messages from the imaginary Frankie.

IN THE KNOW

Full name: **Louis William Tomlinson**
Birth date: **December 24, 1991**
Hometown: **Doncaster, England**
Zodiac sign: **Capricorn**

In his spare time, Louis likes to play soccer. He was invited to join his hometown team, the Doncaster Rovers, as a reserve. Football, as soccer is called in the UK, is a big part of Louis's life. "I have been a massive football fan for a long time and growing up in Doncaster, I've been to plenty of games. To be part of the club is incredible." (*92Live*)

LIAM PAYNE

Lookin' sharp.

Ever since he was five years old, according to The Hits Radio, Liam dreamed of becoming a professional singing star. Growing up, he performed karaoke songs for his family—they couldn't believe his talent. He studied music technology in school, and was also interested in sports. He studied boxing, and trained as a runner.

IN THE KNOW

Full name: Liam James Payne
Birth date: August 29, 1993
Hometown: Wolverhampton, England
Zodiac sign: Virgo

Striking a pose on stage in Buenos Aires, Argentina.

Liam was only fourteen when he first appeared on *The X Factor* in the UK as a solo performer. He was told he was too young, and to return in two years. When he did, he sang so beautifully he received a standing ovation. He didn't win as a soloist, but was chosen by Simon Cowell to join a new group—One Direction!

How does Liam feel about 1D's amazing success? "It's been incredible, but I think it's a credit to the power of our fans more than anything. They're an amazing force." (Billboard)

ZAYN MALIK

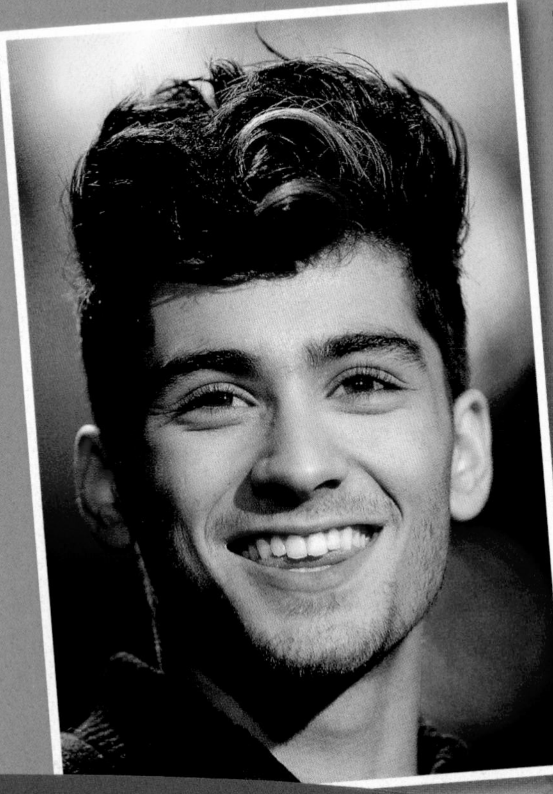

Zayn was interested in acting when he was growing up. He took performing arts classes and acted in school productions. But he had to overcome a bit of stage fright when he appeared on *The X Factor* in the UK. We're glad he did!

Zayn is engaged to Little Mix singer Perrie Ewards, and her 99-year-old great-grandmother Jenny Gaston may be his oldest fan. "Zayn is absolutely lovely," she told the *Daily Mail*. "I love One Direction."

IN THE KNOW

Full name: **Zain Javadd Malik**
Stage name: **Zayn**
Birth date: **January 12, 1993**
Hometown: **Bradford, England**
Zodiac sign: **Capricorn**

Didja know?

Zayn has an unusual way to prepare for a performance—he brushes his teeth!

Zayn was named Best Dressed Male by GQ.

Zayn kept up so well with professional Bollywood dancers during the 1D Day YouTube event, you'd think he'd been dancing all his life.

NIALL HORAN

Niall was into music growing up, and he's an accomplished guitar player. He plays guitar on tour and on 1D's *Midnight Memories* album. He likes playing quite a lot. "Someone told me the smile on my face gets bigger when I play the guitar," he confided to *Billboard*.

When 1D played a series of concerts in Ireland in May 2014, Niall got to enjoy a visit with his family. "I'm excited, I'm nervous, I'm emotional," his mum gushed to RTÉ Radio 1.

IN THE KNOW

Full name: **Niall James Horan**
Birth date: **September 13, 1993**
Hometown: **Mullingar, Ireland**
Zodiac sign: **Virgo**

Didja know?

Niall sang in a church choir when he was growing up.

Niall playing the guitar on *The Today Show*.

AUSTIN MAHONE

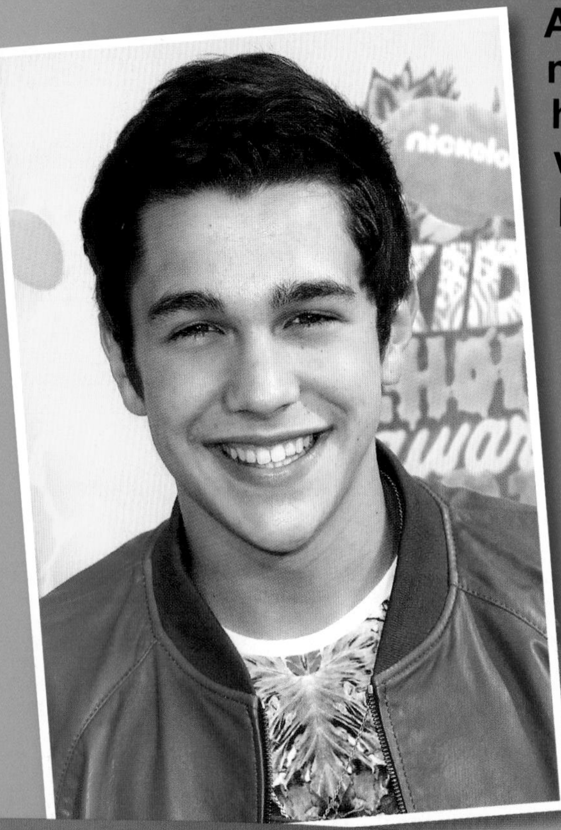

Austin was born in Texas, where his mother brought him up alone after his dad passed away when he was very young. He got his musical start posting music videos on YouTube in 2010, and signed a record deal in 2012. A year later, Austin was on tour as an opening act for Taylor Swift's "Red Tour," and playing guest roles on TV shows like *Big Time Rush* and *The Millers*. In 2013, he won a Radio Disney Music Award as "Breakout Star" and an MTV Video Music Award award as "Artist to Watch," along with two big MTV Awards in Europe. Austin is headlining MTV's "Artists to Watch" tour in 2014.

IN THE KNOW

Full name: **Austin Mahone**
Birth date: **April 4, 1996**
Hometown: **San Antonio, Texas**
Zodiac sign: **Aries**

Austin getting instrumental in concert in Philadelphia.

Austin rocks the house for his loyal "Mahomies," as his fans are called.

Didja know?

Austin has many musical talents. Not only does he sing and play the guitar, but he also plays piano and the drums.

Look who got slimed! The audience at the 2014 Kids' Choice Awards voted on which hot young stars to slime, and Austin was a fave.

THE GUYS OF R5

Ross, Rocky, Rydel, and Riker Lynch grew up in Colorado, where they attended a performing arts school and loved to put on shows for their family. The family moved to Los Angeles, where the kids had success with acting and dance opportunities. With Rocky, Ross and Riker on guitar, and Rydel on keyboards, all they needed was a drummer to form a band. When they met Ellington Ratliff and became best buds, R5 began.

"We just want to go out there and give everybody the time of their lives," Riker told MTV.com.

Rydel Lynch gets to do what every R5 fan dreams about. She rocks out with her brothers Riker, Rocky, Ross, and their friend Ellington ... the guys of R5.

R5's debut single, "Loud," and their first album, *Louder*, came out in 2013, and was soon followed by a hot music video. With their first-ever concert tour and a performance at the White House in 2014, what could R5 do to top that? They have a new album in the works—can't wait!

RIKER LYNCH

Riker is the oldest of the five Lynch kids. It was his interest in pursuing acting and singing that brought the family to Los Angeles, and Riker has realized both dreams. Not only is he one of the lead singers and the bass player for R5, he's done some cool acting, too. Riker has had a recurring role as one of the Dalton Academy Warblers on Fox's hit show *Glee*. He joined the "Glee Live! In Concert!" tour in 2011 and was in *Glee: The 3D Concert Movie*.

Didja know?

If he couldn't be a musician, Riker would want to be a hockey player.

IN THE KNOW

Full name: **Riker Anthony Lynch**
Birth date: **November 8, 1991**
Hometown: **Littleton, Colorado**
Zodiac sign: **Scorpio**

Riker with his fellow Warblers.

ELLINGTON RATLIFF

What is it like being a drummer for one of the hottest bands around? According to Ellington Ratliff, scheduling is the group's toughest issue. "It works out because we live together, so we're together most of the time." (*Vancouver Sun*)

Ratliff is a really fun, easygoing guy, and he told Radio Disney that he likes to think of himself as the funny guy in the band. He also shared that his favorite R5 song is "One Last Dance" because it reminds him of The Beatles, one of his musical inspirations.

Didja know?

Ratliff's favorite food is sushi!

IN THE KNOW

Full name: Ellington Lee Ratliff
Nickname: Ratliff (the fifth "R")
Birth date: April 14, 1993
Hometown: Los Angeles, California
Zodiac sign: Aries

Ratliff rocking out in London.

ROCKY LYNCH

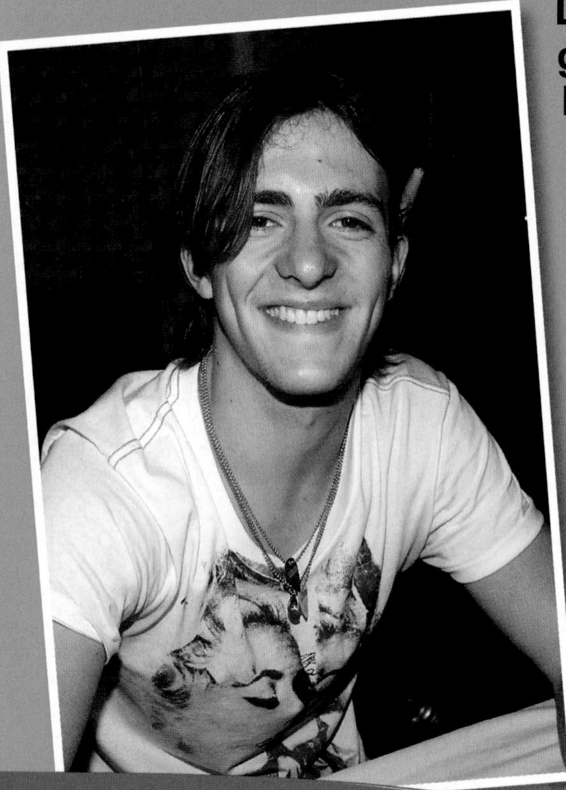

Like his brothers and sister, Rocky grew up performing. "When we were little, our mom always called us 'R4.' We were always singing and dancing," he told *Time for Kids*. Rocky was the first to learn to play guitar, and he taught his brothers how to play as well. He is not only one of the lead guitarists for R5, he writes many of the songs they perform. His favorite R5 song is "Ain't No Way We're Goin' Home."

IN THE KNOW

Full name: **Rocky Lynch**
Birth date: **November 1, 1994**
Hometown: **Littleton, Colorado**
Zodiac sign: **Scorpio**

Doing what he does best: performing for his fans.

Didja know?

Rocky's favorite food is mac 'n' cheese!

ROSS LYNCH

xoxo

Ross may have the busiest schedule of all the guys of R5. Not only does he sing and play rhythm guitar in the group, he stars in the Disney Channel's original series *Austin & Ally*. His performance as teen singer Austin Moon earned him a Nickelodeon Teen Choice Award for Favorite TV Actor two years in a row. He was also in *Teen Beach Movie* and will reprise his role in *Teen Beach Movie 2* in 2015.

IN THE KNOW

Full name: **Ross Shor Lynch**
Birth date: **December 29, 1995**
Hometown: **Littleton, Colorado**
Zodiac sign: **Capricorn**

Ross says:

"I can't not play a guitar if I have a guitar in my hand, I have to play it!"
(Mirror.co.uk)

Didja know?

"Awesome" is his favorite word—and that's just what Ross is!

BROMANCE

All work and no play? No way! Your fave co-stars and band mates aren't all business—they hang out together in real life, too. Check it out.

Teen Wolf's Tyler Hoechlin and Dylan O'Brien hanging out together at the 2013 Young Hollywood Awards.

1D-mates Liam Payne and Niall Horan catching an NBA game together in New York.

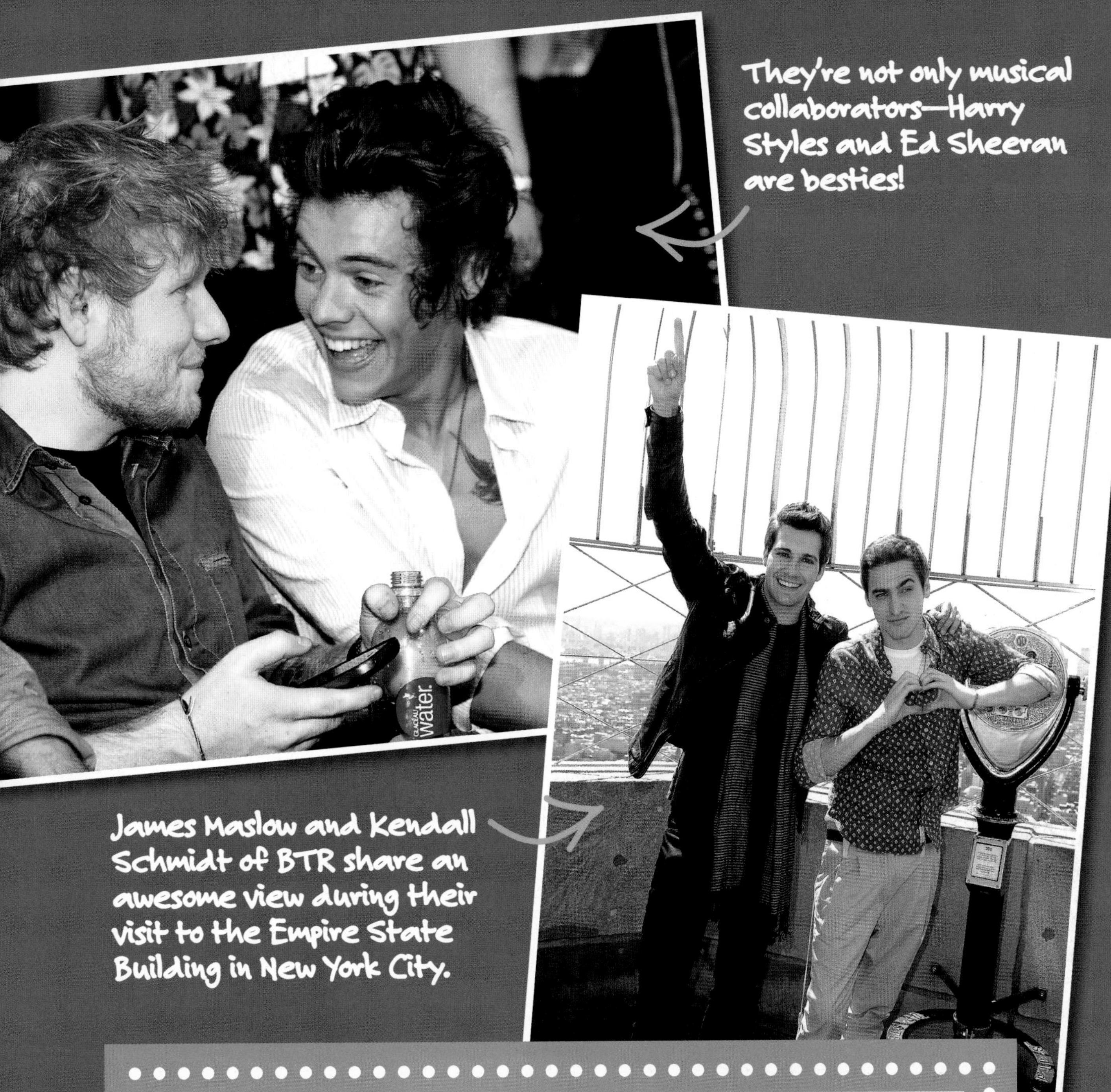

They're not only musical collaborators—Harry Styles and Ed Sheeran are besties!

James Maslow and Kendall Schmidt of BTR share an awesome view during their visit to the Empire State Building in New York City.

Sam Claflin gives Josh Hutcherson a big hug—or is it a noogie?—as they celebrate their MTV Movie Award win. Their *Hunger Games* co-star Jennifer Lawrence talked to MTV about Josh and Sam's friendship: "It's a full-blown bromance . . . it's really adorable."

JACK GRIFFO

Jack has been acting since he was a little kid—he was in a commercial when he was only two years old. His older brothers were into performing, and watching them act in plays inspired Jack. He auditioned for a local community theater company and was cast in productions of *A Christmas Story* and *To Kill a Mockingbird*. His family moved to Los Angeles in 2010.

Jack's guest appearances on popular shows include *Kickin' It*, *Jessie*, and *Marvin Marvin*. An appearance on *See Dad Run* led to his breakout role as Max Thunderman on Nickelodeon's hit TV show *The Thundermans*. He was nominated for a Nickelodeon Kids' Choice Award as "Favorite TV Actor" in 2014 for his work on the show. "I'm blown away by the nomination! Just to be recognized at all when the show is so new is amazing," he told *JustJaredJr.com*.

IN THE KNOW

Full name: **Jack Davis Griffo**
Birth date: **December 11, 1996**
Hometown: **Orlando, Florida**
Zodiac sign: **Sagittarius**

Getting involved at a Power of Youth event.

Didja know?

Jack loves being an actor because actors get to "tell stories and be a part of them." (*blog.scholastic.com*)

BLAKE JENNER

At first, Blake wanted to be a stand-up comic. "I'm definitely in love with improv and comedy," he told *TVLine*. Inspired by Jim Carrey in the movie *Dumb and Dumber*, Blake began pursuing his dream of acting in middle school and high school productions. Interested in learning more and improving his performance abilities, Blake studied acting and improv as well. It must've worked, because before long he was appearing in commercials.

Blake getting the star treatment on *The Glee Project*.

IN THE KNOW

Full name: **Blake Jenner**
Birth date: **August 27, 1992**
Hometown: **Miami, Florida**
Zodiac sign: **Virgo**
Fun fact: **Blake worked in a parrot shop before joining the cast of *Glee*.**

After graduating, Blake moved to Los Angeles. While working to support himself, he studied improv with the famous group The Groundlings—whose alums include Will Ferrell and Kristen Wiig—and got a chance to perform with the group. He was one of fourteen contestants on *The Glee Project*, a reality show whose prize is a role on *Glee*. He won! Blake was guaranteed seven episodes, but the fans spoke and voted him the Teen Choice Award winner for "Breakout Star"—and Blake's character, Ryder Lynn, became a *Glee* series regular.

HUNGER HOTTIES

The *Hunger Games* movies are on fire, and so are the amazing actors who star in the films.

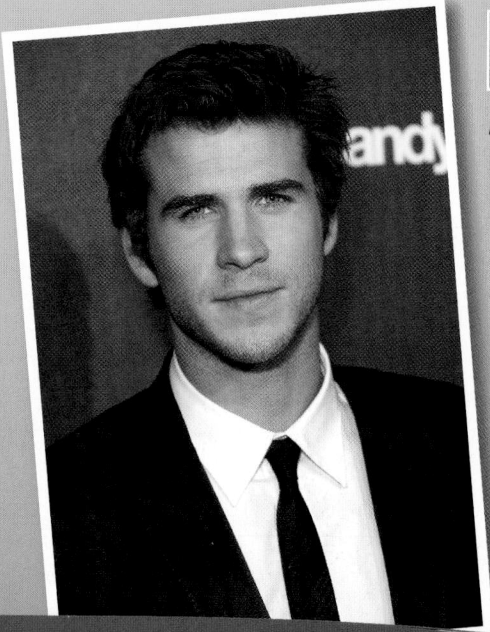

Liam starred in the thriller *Paranoia*, in addition to *Hunger Games: Catching Fire*, in 2013. With his upcoming role as Gale Hawthorne in the two *Hunger Games: Mockingjay* films, he's one busy guy! And we're not surprised that he's on *Glamour* UK's "Sexiest Men" list at number three (2013). Way to go, Liam!

IN THE KNOW

Full name: **Liam Hemsworth**
Birth date: **January 13, 1990**
Hometown: **Phillip Island, Australia**
Zodiac sign: **Capricorn**

xoxo

During Liam's appearance on *Late Night with Jimmy Fallon*, Jimmy made him race motor scooters to compete for the "Hemsworth Cup," which he totally won!

Josh identifies with his character, Peeta Mellark. In fact, when *MTV.com* asked him how he differed from his character, Josh said, "Honestly, we're very similar in so many ways it's kind of hard to pick out the difference." He may not work in a bakery, but he told *InStyle* he makes a good apple pie—"the whole shebang, including the crust." What's he up to now? He's working on the animated Marvel/Disney superhero movie, *Big Hero 6*.

IN THE KNOW

Full name: **Joshua Ryan Hutcherson**
Nickname: **Josh**
Birth date: **October 12, 1992**
Hometown: **Union, Kentucky**
Zodiac sign: **Aquarius**
Loves to: **Play soccer**

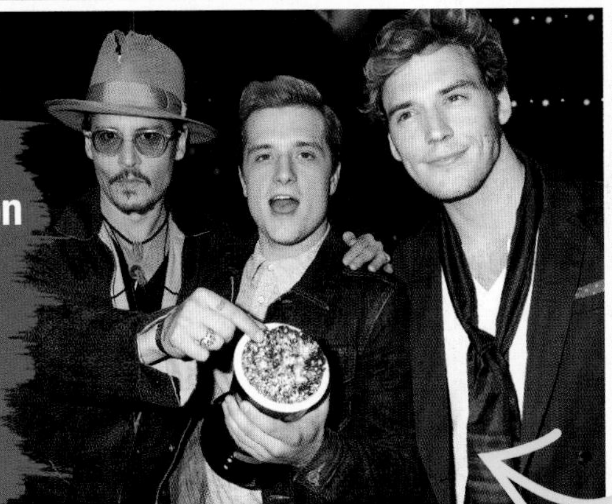

Watch out, Josh and Sam! Looks like Johnny Depp wants a bit of that *Hunger Games: Catching Fire* MTV Movie Award!

Sam transformed himself physically into his athletic *Hunger Games* character, Finnick Odair, through months and months of training and working out. But he didn't need any help relating to the sensitive side of the character. He married his sweetheart, Laura Haddock, in 2013. Sigh!

Sam gets animated while talking to fans at a "Meet the Actor" event in New York City.

IN THE KNOW

Full name: **Samuel George Claflin**
Nickname: **Sam**
Birth date: **June 27, 1986**
Hometown: **Ipswich, England**
Zodiac sign: **Cancer**

BEHIND THE SCENES

Ever wonder what the Hunger Hotties are up to when they're not on set? Check it out!

Bro time! Liam attended the 2014 *Vanity Fair* Oscar Party with his two actor brothers, Luke (middle) and Chris (right).

Alan Ritchson—Gloss in *Catching Fire*—sitting near Lady Gaga at the Versace show at Paris Fashion Week 2014.

Fan favorite Alexander Ludwig followed up his performance as Cato in the first *Hunger Games* movie by playing a Navy SEAL in *Lone Survivor.* And he brought his physical skills to the role of football running back Chris Ryan in the summer 2014 film inspired by a true story, *When the Game Stands Tall.*

Dayo Okeniyi lookin' sharp at the May 2014 premiere of his new comedy film, *Cavemen*. What a transition from his role as the quiet, serious Thresh! Look for him in the new *Terminator* film, coming out in 2015.

Liam, Jen, and Josh were on hand and suitably chic at the Cannes Film Festival 2014.

GARRETT CLAYTON

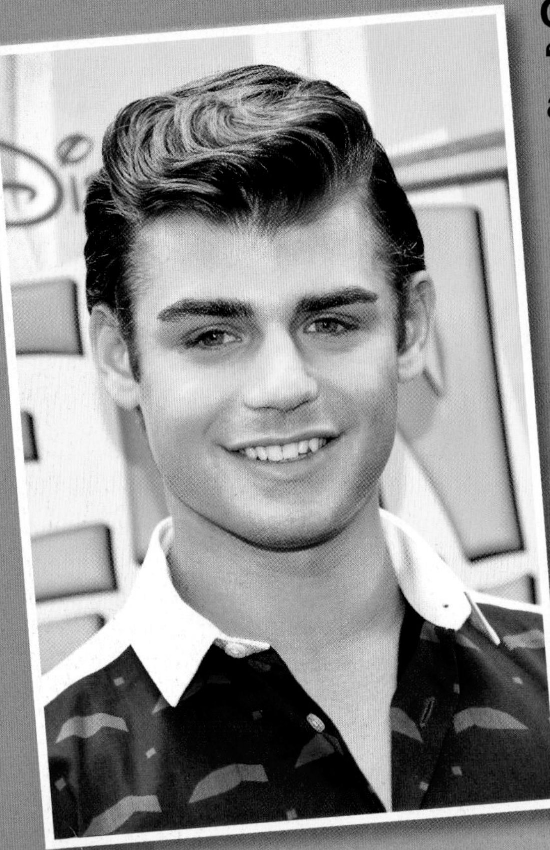

Garrett has amazing green-blue eyes. "It's usually the first thing people notice about me," he told *People* magazine. He's best known for his role as cool surfer Tanner in Disney's *Teen Beach Movie*, and he has a recurring role on *The Fosters*.

Garrett got interested in acting when he was at summer camp and was cast as Uncle Homer in *Charlotte's Web*, but it was his first starring role in his high school's production of *Peter Pan* that got him hooked.

What's up next for Garrett? He'll be reprising his role as Tanner in *Teen Beach Movie 2* in 2015.

IN THE KNOW

Full name: **Gary Clayton**
Stage name: **Garrett**
Birth date: **March 19, 1991**
Hometown: **Dearborn Heights, Michigan**
Zodiac sign: **Pisces**

Garrett with his *Teen Beach Movie* co-stars at Disneyland. Some say he looks like Zac Efron: what do you think?

Didja know?

Garrett's favorite movie is *Back to the Future*. "Hanging out with Marty McFly and Doc Brown would be awesome," he told *Seventeen*.

JADEN SMITH

Jaden's family ties—his parents are Will and Jada Pinkett Smith—may have gotten him interested in acting, but he's made his own way, auditioning for roles and giving knockout performances. Jaden made his movie debut acting opposite his father in *The Pursuit of Happyness*. His performance earned him an MTV Movie Award for Breakthrough Appearance. He followed up with a role in *The Day the Earth Stood Still* and played opposite Jackie Chan in *The Karate Kid*. Next up? Jaden will reprise his role in *The Karate Kid 2* in 2015.

IN THE KNOW

Full name: **Jaden Christopher Syre Smith**
Birth date: **July 8, 1998**
Hometown: **Malibu, California**
Zodiac sign: **Cancer**

Jaden is a designer—he and friends created a clothing line called Msfts.

In addition to being an actor, Jaden is a musician and a dancer. Jaden believes in giving back, and he is a youth ambassador for Project Zambia along with his older half brother Trey and younger sister Willow.

SURF'S UP!

Who can resist a day in the sun on a beautiful beach? Certainly not these stars. Having time off means having bodacious fun when they hit the beach.

A perfect day for Kellan Lutz's swimwear photo shoot.

The guys of Midnight Red enjoy daylight fun in the sun!

Alexander Ludwig rocks the house at the Victoria's Secret Ultimate Spring Break Dance Party in Miami.

Watch out! Looks like Harry Styles has some mad beach volleyball skills.

Ross Lynch rocks a perfect beach look.

DIVERGENT DUDES

The action-packed Divergent book series made a splash on film screens worldwide when the first movie based on the books was released. While the film features a lead female character, Beatrice "Tris" Prior, played by Shailene Woodley, it also includes three amazing young actors: Theo James, Ben Lloyd-Hughes, and Ansel Elgort.

Theo was born in Oxfordshire, England, and is the youngest of five kids. He was in several memorable roles before landing the starring role as Four in *Divergent*, including playing a diplomat in *Downton Abbey* and a vampire in *Underworld: The Awakening.* Theo told *Screenrant.com* he wanted to play the role because of Four's "complexity as a character. He doesn't have to be the loudest voice in the room but he's also someone with presence and someone that you notice."

IN THE KNOW

Full name: **Theo James**
Birth date: **December 16, 1984**
Hometown: **Oxford, England**
Zodiac sign: **Sagittarius**
Fun Fact: **His birth name is Theo Taptiklis**

Making time for fans

Ben is also from England, where he portrayed the character Josh in the British series *Skins*. But playing a character from the United States, Tris's friend Will, in *Divergent* was really tough for Ben, who had never done an American accent in a film before. "I was very aware of it and thought about it all the time," he told *New York Daily News.*

IN THE KNOW

Full name: Benedict Lloyd-Hughes
Nickname: Ben
Birth date: April 14, 1988
Hometown: London, England
Loves to: Read
Zodiac sign: Aries

xoxo

Model-perfect look on the red carpet.

Ansel has been very busy. In addition to landing the role of Caleb opposite Shailene Woodley in the movie *Divergent*, he co-stars with her as Augustus Waters in *The Fault in Our Stars*. Just twenty years old, this super-hunky star with the smoldering stare has become one of the hottest leading men in Hollywood.

Ansel told *Vogue* that when he was little his dad, a photographer, would include him in a shoot "if they needed an extra." He got a taste of the spotlight from an early age, but learned that "if you're not the star, then your job is to not pull attention away from the star." Very wise.

Ansel also moonlights as a music producer and DJ, using the name Ansolo. His first recording, "Unite," came out in April 2014. He describes his style as "clubby and groovy." Look for more from this talented newcomer.

IN THE KNOW

Full name: Ansel Elgort
Nickname: Ansolo
Birth date: March 14, 1994
Hometown: New York, New York
Zodiac sign: Pisces

CODY SIMPSON

When Cody was growing up, he listened to his dad play guitar and sing at family parties. This inspired Cody, and when he was just seven years old he got interested in playing guitar and writing songs. Just a few years later, Cody began performing popular songs and his own music on YouTube and performing in public. His YouTube channel got millions of views, and he was soon discovered by a US-based record producer—it now has nearly 200 million views!

Wowing some lucky fans on stage at the Radio Disney Music Awards.

IN THE KNOW

Full name: **Cody Robert Simpson**
Birth date: **January 11, 1997**
Hometown: **Gold Coast, Queensland, Australia**
Zodiac sign: **Capricorn**

AN AWARD-WINNING PERFORMER!

- Nickelodeon Kids' Choice Awards in 2012, 2013, and 2014.
- Young Hollywood Role Model Award in 2013.
- Three Nickelodeon Australian Kids' Choice Awards in 2011.

Early success with his first Aussie Kid's Choice Award in 2010.

In 2010, Cody signed with Atlantic Records, moved to Los Angeles with his family, joined the "Camplified" tour across the US, and had a number one Radio Disney hit song, "All Day." And that was just the beginning! When Cody's EP, *Coast to Coast*, was released, it hit the Billboard chart at number twelve, and his musical career has skyrocketed ever since. Cody's debut studio album was called *Paradise*, and his second album, *Surfer's Paradise*, debuted in the top ten on Billboard's Hot 200 chart.

Didja know?

Cody was a competitive swimmer when he was growing up, and he won two gold medals at the Queensland Swimming Championships.

Cody showing off his dance moves in concert in London.

THE VAMPS

The British band The Vamps was born on the Internet when guitarist James McVey and lead singer Bradley Simpson met through YouTube. As Brad told *The Telegraph*, "Bands used to form through an advert . . . but now it's amazing what you can find on YouTube." The two guys began by writing music together. They found an awesome drummer, Tristan Evans, through an audition tape. All they needed then to form the band was a great bass player. A friend introduced them to Connor Ball, and The Vamps were born.

The Vamps have played opening acts on Taylor Swift's "Red Tour" and R5's "Louder World Tour." Since then, their popularity has skyrocketed. Their debut single, "Can We Dance," landed at number two on the British singles chart, and they began headlining their own "Meet The Vamps" tour in 2014.

RED CARPET *Swagger*

It's simple elegance for Kellan Lutz at the Oscars.

Avan Jogia lets his hair down at the Kids' Choice Awards.

Roshon Fegan shows off his funky fashion sense at the Grammy Awards.

Whether they go the formal route or take a different path, these guys always look like winners. Some set their own personal style, and others work with stylists. Everyone wants to look good when they walk the red carpet.

Ansel Elgort shows his elegant side on the red carpet ar the MTV Movie Awards.

The guys of 1D look like they're trying to steal the show—or something else—at the 2014 BRIT Awards.

On a break from touring with One Direction, 5 Seconds of Summer's Michael Clifford, Calum Hood, Luke Hemmings, and Ashton Irwin have some fun on the red carpet at the BRIT Awards. 5SOS won the Nickelodeon Kids' Choice Award for "Aussies' Fave New Talent" in 2014.

MIDNIGHT RED

Joey Diggs, Jr. is from Los Angeles, California. Colton Rudloff is from Buffalo, New York. Eric Secharia is from Valencia, California. Thomas Augusto is from Arlington, Texas. And Anthony Ladao is from Seattle, Washington. But they all come together onstage as Midnight Red. They got a big break when they joined the New Kids on the Block/Backstreet Boys co-headline tour as opening act in 2011, and that was just the beginning for this talented group of guys.

"We've learned how everyone works and what their strengths are, so now we sing better together and dance better together. That dynamic between us just keeps getting stronger and stronger," Thomas told MTV.com.

Midnight Red is featured with Austin Mahone on MTV's "Artist to Watch" tour. And their first digital single, "One Club At A Time," was an instant hit when it was chosen as one of three songs to be featured on *So You Think You Can Dance* on National Dance Day.

WHAT'S IN A NAME

"One night I had a dream, and it told me to use the word midnight*. Then as a group we decided to add the word* red *on the end of it, to pay homage to our producer* RedOne *. . . Midnight is a fun hour, everybody wants to stay out past midnight, party hour. And red is a very dominant color. And we want to dominate,"* Joey *explained to* Crushable.com.

FACE TIME

COLTON RUDLOFF

JOEY DIGGS, JR.

ERIC SECHARIA

ANTHONY LADAO

THOMAS AUGUSTO

DISTINCTIVE LOCKS

"People are like, 'How get your hair to do tha it's always been natur big. I hated it when I w kid. But I've since set to do its own thing," T *told the* Star-Telegram

Heartthrob HAIRSTYLES

FLOWING LOCKS!

ROSS LYNCH

LOUIS TOMLINSON

The long and the short of it!

DOUGLAS BOOTH

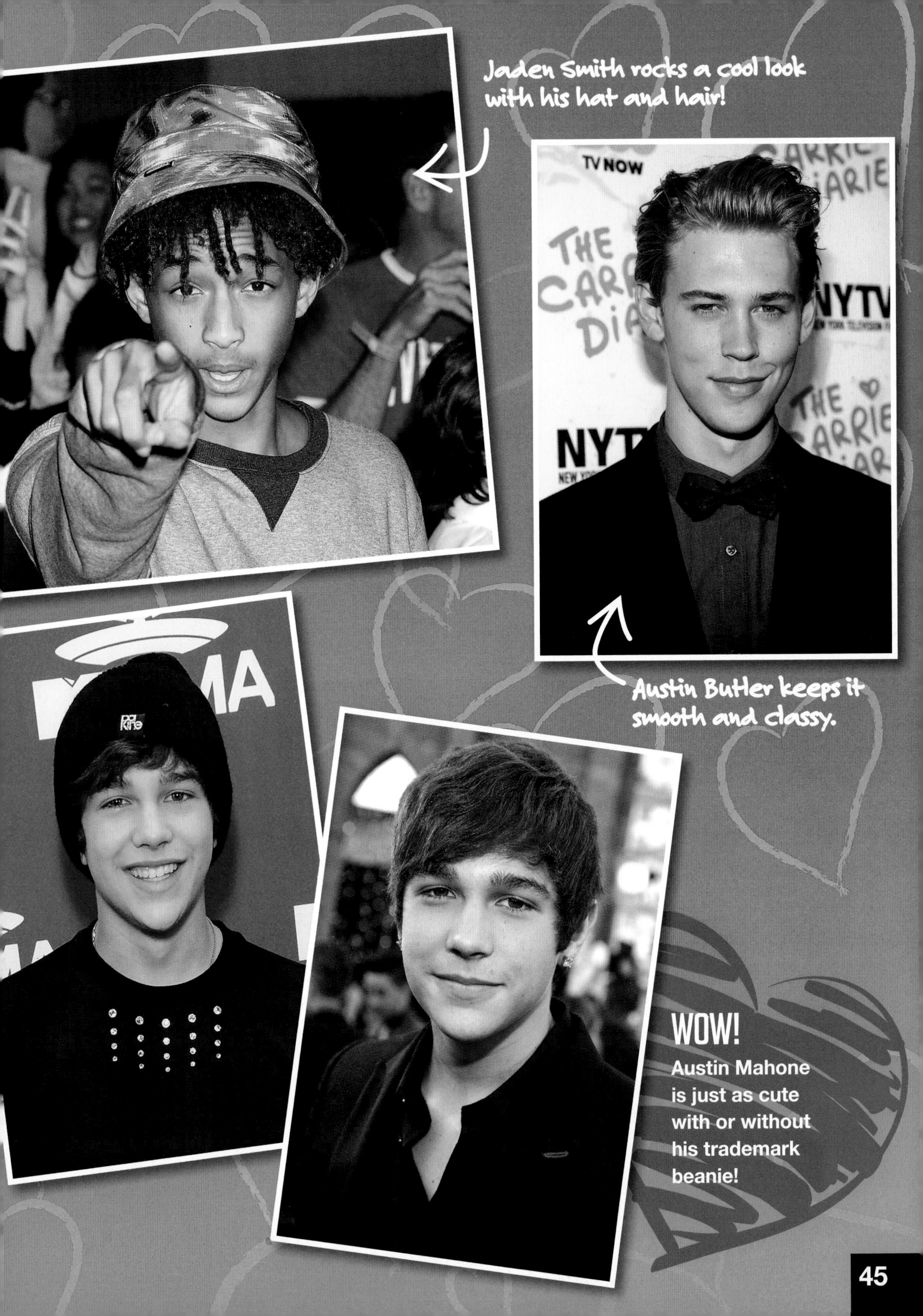

Jaden Smith rocks a cool look with his hat and hair!

Austin Butler keeps it smooth and classy.

WOW!

Austin Mahone is just as cute with or without his trademark beanie!

BAND-TASTIC

First the red carpet is rolled out. Then fans and photographers arrive. Finally, limousines pull up and the coolest musicians step out. What could be more exciting than that? A live performance by your fave! Here are some bands and artists that take home the award for most awesome performance at an awards show.

1D's "Best Song Ever" won "Best Song of the Summer" at the MTV Video Music Awards in 2013.

Austin Mahone was on point at the 2013 Radio Disney Music Awards.

Big Time Rush wowed the crowd at the Mexico Kids' Choice Awards in 2013.

5SOS rocked the house in their debut appearance at the 2014 Billboard Music Awards.

Ed Sheeran performed a duet of his song "The A Team" with music legend Elton John at the Grammy Awards in 2013.

NOLAN GOULD

Nolan began acting in commercials when he was three years old. Since then, he has transformed from a little cutie to a total hottie. Nolan's mad acting skills have range: he made us tremble as a boy living in a town terrorized by monsters in the horror flick *Ghoul*, and makes us smile as accident-prone Luke Dunphy on the TV show *Modern Family.*

IN THE KNOW

Full name: **Nolan Gould**
Birth date: **October 28, 1998**
Hometown: **New York, New York**
Zodiac sign: **Scorpio**
Loves to: **Play banjo**

SMART GUY!

Nolan is a member of Mensa, an organization for people with high IQs. He graduated from high school when he was thirteen years old.

CHILL!

Nolan is a youth ambassador for the Sierra Club, and is spotted here at one of their holiday events.

WILD SIDE!

Nolan and *Modern Family* co-star Rico Rodriguez at the Wild Life Sydney Zoo in Australia.

ROSHON FEGAN

Roshon has some serious skills as a performer. He can sing, dance, and play the drums, guitar, and piano. He brought all of his talents together for his role as Ty Blue, Rocky Blue's cool, talented older brother, on *Shake it Up!* He won two Young Artist Awards for his work on the show.

Even though he was already a dancer, Roshon said he was still challenged by his time learning ballroom moves on *Dancing with the Stars*. "Most people have a blank slate and can start from nothing. But for me, I had to break a bad habit that I've been doing all of my life, which is freestyle hip-hop," he told *Parade.com*.

IN THE KNOW

Full name: Roshon Fegan
Nickname: RO SHON
Birth date: October 6, 1991
Hometown: Los Angeles, California
Zodiac sign: Libra
Fun Fact: He was in Disney's *Camp Rock*.

Singing and rocking a keytar.

SCHOOL DAZE

Ever wonder what your celebrity crush was like in school? Check out these snaps to see what some of your faves were up to.

Kellan Lutz was a busy boy in high school—not only did he box, he was also in Latin club and French club, and he played on the football team.

Chord Overstreet was a model student. In fact, he told the *Chicago Tribune* that he did some shoots for Gap and Famous Footwear.

Darren Criss was strumming and crooning from the very beginning.

It looks like Austin Mahone liked goofing off with friends. What a cutie!

XOXO

Taylor Lautner showed school spirit while participating in a football game.

THE GUYS OF TWILIGHT

The Twilight Saga was a phenomenally successful book series and movie franchise, and it introduced millions not only to its compelling characters, including Edward and Jacob, but also to the guys who played them. The film series may be complete, but there's a lot more to love about the *Twilight* hunks.

Rob wowed us with his star-making turn as vegetarian vampire Edward in the *Twilight* movies, after winning our hearts as Cedric Diggory in *Harry Potter and the Goblet of Fire*. In addition to his busy acting career, Rob makes time to give back. He supports numerous charitable efforts, from visiting young patients at the Children's Hospital of Los Angeles to donating his time and personal items to the GO Campaign, an organization dedicated to funding projects to help children around the world.

Full name: Robert Douglas Thomas Pattinson
Nickname: Rob
Birth date: May 13, 1986
Hometown: London, England
Zodiac sign: Taurus
Fun Fact: Rob contributed songs to the *Twilight* soundtrack.

xoxo

Saying "hey" at the 2014 Cannes Film Festival.

Taylor started acting when he was a kid doing voiceovers (*Danny Phantom, Scooby-Doo*), and got his big break as Sharkboy in *The Adventures of Sharkboy and Lavagirl in 3-D*. He hadn't heard of the *Twilight* series when he auditioned for the role of Jacob Black, but he nailed it anyway—and we're glad he did! Taylor has a new role starring in the action thriller *Tracers*, set in New York City.

IN THE KNOW

Full name: Taylor Daniel Lautner
Birth date: February 11, 1992
Hometown: Hudsonville, Michigan
Zodiac sign: Aquarius

Showing off his physical skills—and physique—while filming *Tracers* in New York City's Central Park.

Kellan started life in a small town with seven siblings, but he was destined to stand out from the crowd. His role as Emmett Cullen in the *Twilight* films was a big break, and he made the most of it by doing all of his own vampire stunts for the film. Since *Twilight*, Kellan played a very hunky Hercules in *The Legend of Hercules*.

IN THE KNOW

Full name: Kellan Christopher Lutz
Birth date: March 15, 1985
Hometown: Dickinson, North Dakota
Zodiac sign: Pisces
Loves to: Watch horror movies

Happy birthday, Kellan!

SNAPSHOTS

The cast of *Teen Beach Movie* performing in the Christmas Day Parade at Disneyland.

Whoa, Jaden Smith, what do you see?

Uh oh! Here comes some slime-tastic fun for Austin Mahone and Cody Simpson at the 2014 Kid's Choice Awards.

Ian Harding of *Pretty Little Liars* with some cool superheroes at a Race for Every Child event in 2013.

Having Fun! James McVey of The Vamps with a fan.

Here's a *Glee*-ful way to get around—Darren Criss hitches a ride from fellow castmate Chord Overstreet.

Josh Hutcherson spoofing *The Hunger Games* on *SNL*.

Harry Styles struts his stuff for

JAKE T. AUSTIN

Jake began acting in commercials at the age of seven, but he became well known when cast as Max Russo, the youngest sibling on Disney's Emmy Award–winning *Wizards of Waverly Place* with co-stars David Henrie and Selena Gomez. He voiced the character of Fernando in *Rio* and *Rio 2*.

Jake currently co-stars in the ABC Family hour-long drama series, *The Fosters*. Excited about his new show, Jake told *Teen Vogue*, "It's very relatable to everyone. It's a show for parents *and* for kids."

IN THE KNOW

Full name: **Jake Austin Szymanski**
Stage name: **Jake T. Austin**
Birth date: **December 3, 1994**
Hometown: **New York, New York**
Zodiac sign: **Sagittarius**

Jake putting his game face on at the Cartoon Network Hall of Game Awards in 2014.

Didja know?

Jake was the voice of Dora the Explorer's cousin, Diego.

Grateful for his success, Jake is committed to giving back. He has been a youth ambassador for Ronald McDonald House New York. "Anything I can do to give back, I'm up for." (*Glamoholic.com*)

Jake supports the Ronald McDonald House at a Power of Youth event.

Jake presenting the Outstanding Social Activism award to Wilmer Valderrama at the 2013 American Latino Media Awards, also known as the ALMA Awards.

HALF TIME

Whether on set, in the public eye, or enjoying some R&R, these guys always have time to toss a ball, catch a wave, or hit the slopes.

Master of spin? Josh Hutcherson shows off his basketball skills on *Late Night with Jimmy Fallon.*

Wesley Stromberg, along with the other members of Emblem3, skateboarding during a performance.

Kellan Lutz shreds serious snow in Utah.

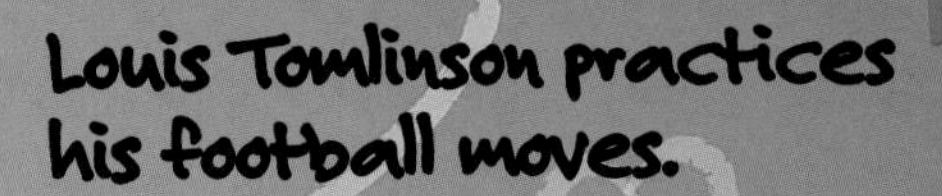

Louis Tomlinson practices his football moves.

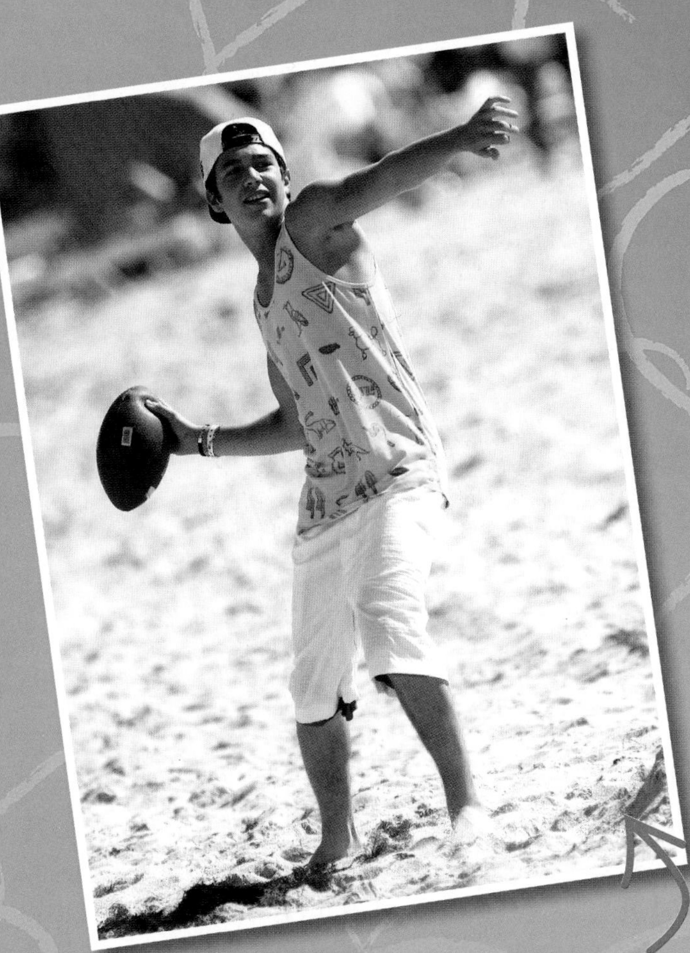

Austin Mahone makes a long toss on the beach in Miami.

Cowabunga, dude! Nolan Gould learns to surf down under.

ED SHEERAN

Ed Sheeran is one of the most talented singer-songwriters in the music biz. Just ask Taylor Swift, who became such a big fan of Ed's that she invited him to join her "Red Tour"—he also wrote the song "Everything Has Changed" for her album, *Red*. Ed has written songs for One Direction, too, including "Moments," "Over Again," and "Little Things."

IN THE KNOW

Full name: **Edward Sheeran**
Nickname: **Ed**
Birth date: **February 17, 1991**
Hometown: **Framlingham, England**
Zodiac sign: **Aquarius**

Ed has been active on the music scene for several years, slowly building his fan base with hundreds of shows a year. In 2011, he became huge on YouTube and a top-selling artist on iTunes, and that was just the beginning. With his incredible talent and adorable smile, Ed's stardom keeps rising.

Ed's love for the guitar first got him into music and singing.

Ed performs with Taylor Swift.

Ed was inspired by listening to The Beatles growing up, and he got to play in a tribute to the four lads at the 2014 Grammy Awards ceremony.

BIG TIME

Big Time Rush broke onto the scene with their own Nickelodeon TV show about the Hollywood lives of four hockey players chosen for a boy band, and it became an instant hit. So did the band members, Kendall Schmidt, James Maslow, Carlos Pena, Jr., and Logan Henderson, the gorgeous stars of BTR.

When the guys of BTR get together on stage, they wow their fans with their amazing music and dancing. They've been nominated for numerous awards, and performed live at Nickelodeon's Worldwide Day of Play.

RUSH

FACE TIME

Most romantic

KENDALL SCHMIDT

Funniest

CARLOS PENA, JR.

Totally focused

JAMES MASLOW

Great problem solver

LOGAN HENDERSON

FAN-demonium

Austin Mahone did a special favor for a Mahomie at a New York show. Her friend couldn't make it to the show, so he called to say hi.

Guess who's a huge *Teen Wolf* fan? None other than the Teen Wolf himself—Tyler Posey! He told *Entertainment Weekly* that when he gets a script for a new episode, "I view it very much as a fan of the show . . . I get really sucked into it."

The Vamps signed copies of their album, *Meet The Vamps,* in Manchester, England, and posed for photos with fans.

Stars know they wouldn't be anywhere without their fans. That's why they love meeting and interacting with the people who helped them get to the top, whether it's at a special event or a chance encounter.

Roshon Fegan signed his EP *I AM ROSHON* for young fans at a meet-and-greet event in New York.

Harry Styles took a break from his pool fun in Miami to sign autographs for some passing Directioners. When 1D won a BRIT Award, Harry said, "A massive thank you to all of our incredible, incredible fans."

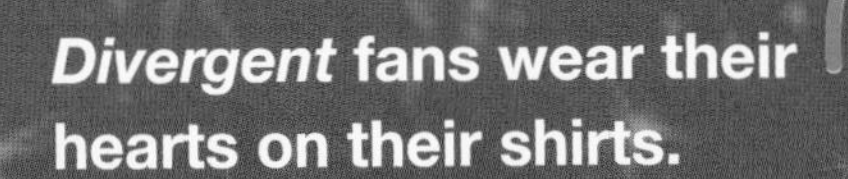

Divergent fans wear their hearts on their shirts.

NOAH CRAWFORD

Noah is just too cute for words! The actor and singer is best known for his turn as Nelson Baxter in *How to Rock,* a part in *The Land of the Lost,* and as the voice of James, son of Black Widow and Captain America, in *Next Avengers: Heroes of Tomorrow.*

IN THE KNOW

Full name: Noah Crawford
Birth date: October 13, 1994
Hometown: Oklahoma City, Oklahoma
Zodiac sign: Libra
Fun Fact: His sisters Hannah, Oliviah and Bellah, are actors, too.

LENDING A HAND

Noah Crawford met with students at the New Horizon Elementary and Middle School when he volunteered as part of Nickelodeon's "The Big Help." He also helped build a garden shed at the school. "The kids were awesome," Noah said. (*CelebSecrets4U.com*)

DOUGLAS BOOTH

Doug has the reading disorder dyslexia and had to work harder than other kids. He says this made him more resilient. How did he get the acting bug? When he was twelve, he played the challenging title role of *Agamemnon*, and knew right away, "This is where I want to be." (*Vogue*)

Doug played Pip in the BBC's *Great Expectations*, a performance critically acclaimed as "haunting." (*Los Angeles Times*) He's been keeping very busy with roles in *Noah*, playing Noah's son Shem, as well as in *Jupiter Ascending* and *The Riot Club*.

IN THE KNOW

Full name: Douglas Booth
Nickname: Doug
Birth date: July 9, 1992
Hometown: London, England
Zodiac sign: Cancer
Loves to: Ski and ride mountain bikes

Romeo, oh, Romeo. It's hard to imagine anyone else but Douglas Booth playing the part of the hopeless romantic in Shakespeare's *Romeo and Juliet.* "When I got that call, it was mad. You don't get that opportunity every day," Doug told *Movieed*. How did he prepare to play Romeo? He worked out with a trainer, and he thought back to the first time he fell in love.

SELFIES!

Even though they get photographed by the press all the time, stars don't mind posing for pics with their amazing fans.

Tyler Posey from Teen Wolf can't resist a pic on the red carpet at the MTV Movie Awards.

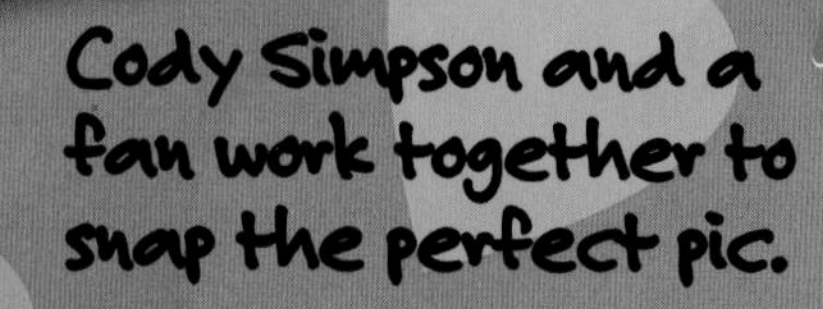

Cody Simpson and a fan work together to snap the perfect pic.

Kendall Schmidt from BTR knows that funny selfies are just as important as serious ones.

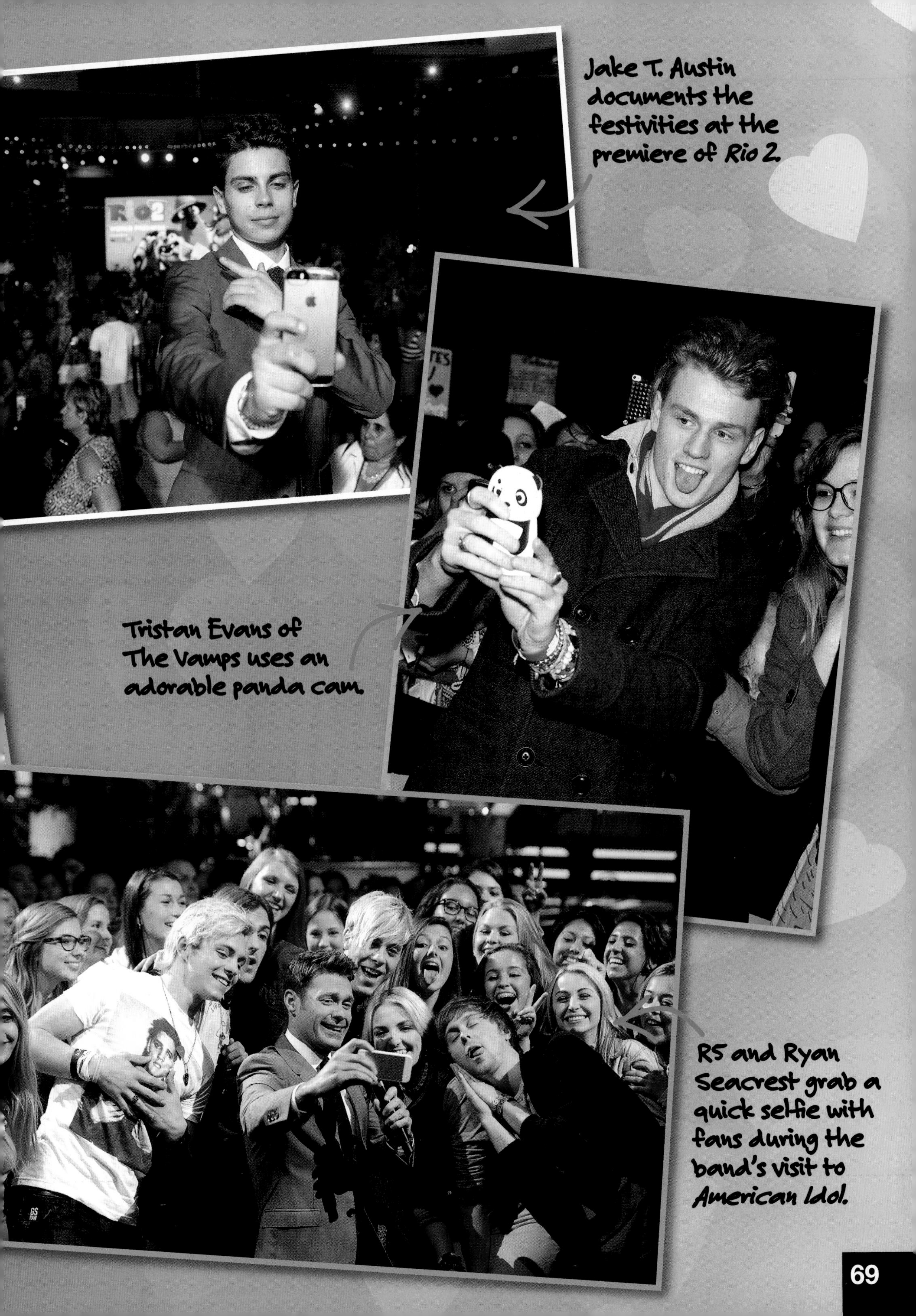

Jake T. Austin documents the festivities at the premiere of *Rio 2*.

Tristan Evans of The Vamps uses an adorable panda cam.

R5 and Ryan Seacrest grab a quick selfie with fans during the band's visit to *American Idol*.

UESS THAT TAT

ell do you know your favorite inked guys? Check out
otos and see if you can guess the star from their tattoo.
rs are at the bottom of the page.

Answer Key: 1. Anthony Ladao 2. Louis Tomlinson
3. Ed Sheeran 4. Zayn Malik 5. Drew Chadwick
6. Harry Styles 7. Liam Payne 8. Kendall Schmidt

4
5
6
7
8

WINNING WAYS

The lads of 1D got a "standing O" when they received the Global Success Award at the 2014 BRIT Awards—their second time receiving this cool award. They also won for their "Best Song Ever" video. Their single "What Makes You Beautiful" won them their first BRIT Award in 2012.

Ross Lynch won "Favorite TV Actor" a second time for his role in *Austin & Ally* at the 2014 Kids' Choice Awards. He made sure to thank all the fans during his acceptance speech, and said that *Austin & Ally* was the best experience ever.

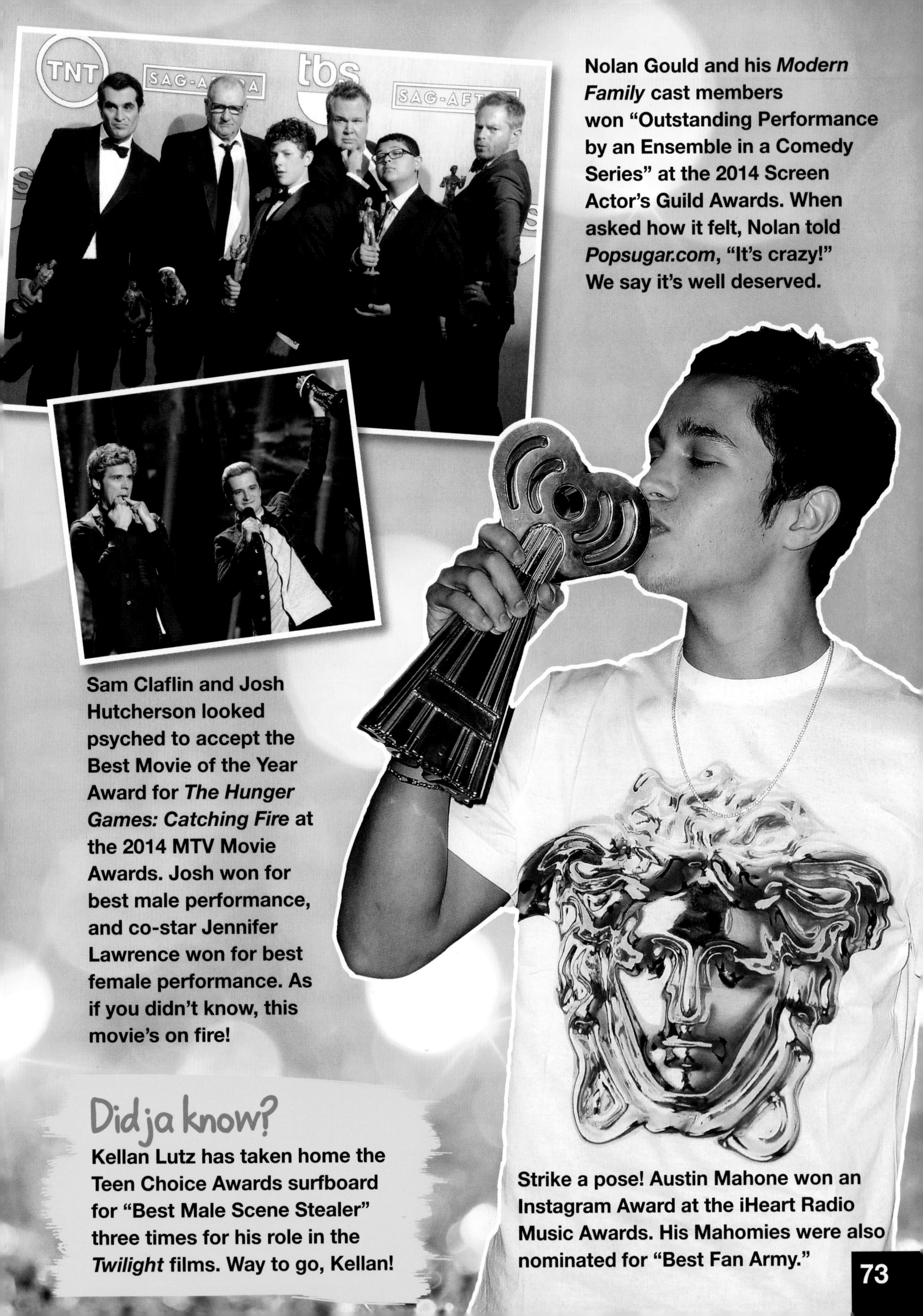

Nolan Gould and his *Modern Family* cast members won "Outstanding Performance by an Ensemble in a Comedy Series" at the 2014 Screen Actor's Guild Awards. When asked how it felt, Nolan told *Popsugar.com*, "It's crazy!" We say it's well deserved.

Sam Claflin and Josh Hutcherson looked psyched to accept the Best Movie of the Year Award for *The Hunger Games: Catching Fire* at the 2014 MTV Movie Awards. Josh won for best male performance, and co-star Jennifer Lawrence won for best female performance. As if you didn't know, this movie's on fire!

Didja know?

Kellan Lutz has taken home the Teen Choice Awards surfboard for "Best Male Scene Stealer" three times for his role in the *Twilight* films. Way to go, Kellan!

Strike a pose! Austin Mahone won an Instagram Award at the iHeart Radio Music Awards. His Mahomies were also nominated for "Best Fan Army."

LEO HOWARD

Leo started studying the martial arts when he was a little kid. "I was four years old, which is a little wacky, because what four-year-old goes out and says 'I want to do karate?'" he said. "But I just had this weird passion for it and I just couldn't get enough." (*OC Register*) He joined a martial arts group that did demonstrations, and that got him hooked on performing.

IN THE KNOW

Full name: Leo Howard
Nickname: Hazard
Birth date: July 13, 1997
Hometown: Fallbrook, California
Zodiac sign: Cancer
Fun Fact: Leo's parents are professional dog breeders, and his dad's nickname is "The Big Bulldog."

Leo's mad martial arts skills came in handy when he auditioned for the role of Jack on *Kickin' It*—he got the part, of course! Whether he is playing a soldier in *GI Joe: The Rise of Cobra*, for which he got to do his own stunts, or as young Conan in *Conan the Barbarian*, or martial arts master Jack on the Disney show *Kickin' It*, Leo is in a class by himself.

Here Leo is showing off his moves at the *G.I. Joe: Retaliation* premiere.

JACOB ARTIST

IN THE KNOW

Full name: **Jacob Artist**
Nickname: **Jake**
Birth date: **October 17, 1992**
Hometown: **Williamsville, New York**
Zodiac sign: **Libra**
Loves to: **Dance ballet**

Jacob has been dancing since the age of five. Trained in jazz, hip-hop, tap, and ballet, he was accepted to the prestigious Julliard School for dance, but turned them down in order to pursue his acting career. That choice is paying off! Jacob was cast as Noah "Puck" Puckerman's half brother, Jake, on *Glee*. There's another reason that Jacob loves to dance, too. "Girls love guys who dance, and I'm definitely going to be the first one on the dance floor," he told *Elle*.

Jacob rocks a blue satin jacket with fellow castmate Blake Jenner.

SPENCER BOLDMAN

You know him as the superpowered Adam Davenport in *Lab Rats,* but Spencer first fell in love with acting when he performed in Shakespeare's *A Midsummer Night's Dream* at his middle school. A teacher had to beg him to audition, but once he hit the stage, he knew what he wanted to do with his life. Since moving to Hollywood, he's landed roles in *iCarly* and *I'm with the Band*, as well as the movie *21 Jump Street* with Channing Tatum and Jonah Hill.

IN THE KNOW

Full name: **Spencer Thomas Boldman**
Birth date: **July 28, 1992**
Hometown: **Plano, Texas**
Zodiac sign: **Leo**
Loves to: **Work out, hike, eat, sleep, and hang with his dog.**

Spencer says:

"I love to read. I was in AP English in high school . . . Moby Dick *and* The Great Gatsby *are two of my favorites."* (Seventeen)

Spencer struts his stuff during a celebrity fashion show at a Race to Erase MS charity event.

NATHAN SYKES

You could say that Nathan was born with music in him: his mom was a music teacher, and he started playing the piano and singing at the age of six. Before he was a teenager, he'd met Britney Spears when he won her competition, "Britney Spears's Karaoke Kriminals." But his real breakthrough came at age sixteen, when he beat out thousands of hopefuls all over England to become the youngest member of The Wanted. American audiences have gotten to know The Wanted boys personally, thanks to their reality show on E!, *The Wanted Life.*

IN THE KNOW

Full name: **Nathan James Sykes**
Birth date: **April 18, 1993**
Hometown: **Gloucester, England**
Zodiac sign: **Aries**
Fun fact: **Nathan's not only the youngest band member, he's also the neatest and most organized.**

Didja know?

After an appearance on *The Tonight Show with Jay Leno*, The Wanted stuck around to sing with their fans outside the studio. Nice!

@NathanTheWanted: "*I am always so happy with my hair at the start of a gig and then by the end of it I just look like a fluffy dog fresh out of a hurricane.*"

SEAN BERDY

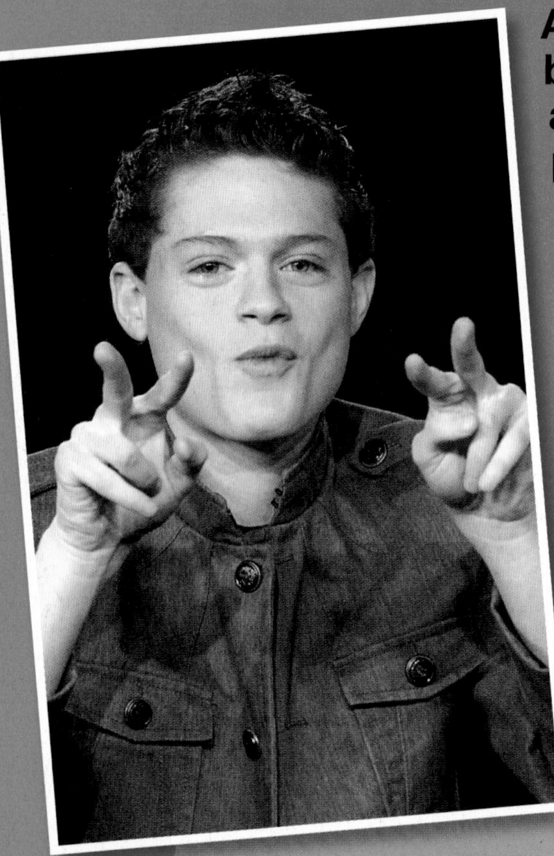

Although Sean has been deaf from birth, he's been communicating to audiences since childhood, when he put on shows with his younger brother for their family and friends in Boca Raton, Florida, and even took up the drums. His first major film role was as the lovable Sammy "Fingers" Samuelson in *The Sandlot 2*, but he is best known for playing the hunky yet sensitive Emmett Bledsoe in the ABC Family TV hit *Switched at Birth*.

IN THE KNOW

Full name: Sean Lance Berdy
Birth date: June 3, 1993
Hometown: Boca Raton, Florida
Zodiac sign: Gemini
Fun fact: Sean's best bud is a bulldog, King Cabo.

A live performer at heart, Sean tours the country when he isn't filming, using American Sign Language in his public appearances and performances. He's working on a one-man show that will incorporate standup comedy and inspiring, true stories from his incredible life.

"As a kid performing, I looked up to Jim Carrey . . . he was one of the big inspirations in my young life, and he still is." (Thetvaddict.com)

Didja know?

As a sophomore at the Indiana School for the Deaf, Sean was named the 2010 Mr. Deaf Teen America.

LUCAS GRABEEL

When Lucas Grabeel started a boys' a cappella singing group at his high school, he never dreamed he'd end up a national sensation. But a few years later, when he landed the role of Ryan Evans in *High School Musical*, that's exactly what happened. An all-around talent, Lucas can play drums, guitar, and accordion, dance in every style you can think of—including ballet—and act and sing up a storm. In 2009, he was voted "Most Likely to Do Big Things" by MTV. If going on to star in the hit ABC Family series *Switched at Birth* is any indication, they were absolutely right.

IN THE KNOW

Full name: **Lucas Stephen Grabeel**
Birth date: **November 23, 1984**
Hometown: **Springfield, Missouri**
Zodiac sign: **Sagittarius**
Loves to: **Dance ballet**

Didja know?

When he's not working, Lucas likes to listen to music, draw, and paint.

Lucas says:

"Once I got on stage and saw the audience, I realized this was what I wanted to do for the rest of my life." (TeenInk)

LIDS & SHADES

Adorable twelve-year-old Leo Howard wasn't afraid of a bold fedora look.

I see you! Avan Jogia peers over his shades at the *Iron Man 3* premiere.

Austin Mahone is famous for his love of beanies, but he also loves to rock a backwards snapback to match his colorful outfits.

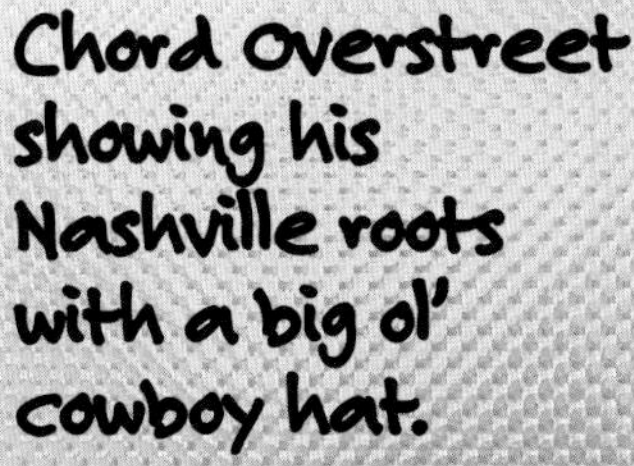

Chord Overstreet showing his Nashville roots with a big ol' cowboy hat.

Cody Simpson is a hat guy, too. In fact, he's on a hat so that his fans, the "Simpsonizers," can proclaim their love for the singer wherever they go.

Jaden Smith wears some out-of-this-world alien shades to the MTV Video Music Awards.

JUST LIKE US

They may sometimes lead glamorous lives, but guys we love enjoy casual fun and run errands during downtime, just like us.

Harry Styles goes hiking on a day off during a 1D South American tour.

Cody Simpson rocks casual jeans while leaving a DWTS practice session.

Logan Henderson of BTR strolling in NYC.

Austin Butler gets into the spirit of things at the Coachella music festival 2014.

Taylor Lautner enjoys himself at a UCLA basketball game.

Colton Haynes takes a coffee on the go while doing Christmas shopping with a friend at The Grove in California.

Jaden Smith checks out the merchandise at a gem and minerals store in West Hollywood.

CAMERON BOYCE

Ever since Cameron's first appearance on TV at age six, in a Panic! at the Disco music video, he's been working steadily on television and in movies. He may be most well-known for his comical turn as Adam Sandler's super-spoiled son in the comedy *Grown Ups*. In 2011, Cameron was cast as the mischievous Luke Ross in the comedy series *Jessie* on the Disney Channel. He recently joined the cast of the Disney Channel's original film *Descendants*—he's playing Carlos, an evil son of *101 Dalmatians'* Cruella de Vil.

IN THE KNOW

Full name: Cameron Boyce
Birth date: May 28, 1999
Hometown: Los Angeles, California
Zodiac sign: Gemini
Fun fact: Cameron is a member of dance crew X Mob.

Cameron and his *Jessie* co-star Peyton List with First Lady Michelle Obama at the White House Easter Egg Roll in 2014.

"Keep on reading; it's really important, and everybody's job involves reading—including mine. So you have to keep it up!" Cameron told blog.scholastic.com.

AUSTIN BUTLER

It's like a fairy tale! At age thirteen, Austin Butler was walking around the Orange County Fair when he was approached by a talent scout who got him his first acting work. After playing small parts, modeling, and taking classes to develop his acting skills, Austin started landing amazing roles in television. He's acted in *Zoey 101, Wizards of Waverly Place,* and *iCarly*. When he guest-starred on *iCarly*, Austin performed the song "Whatever My Love." He also played a heartthrob in *Switched at Birth*. When he's not breaking hearts on screen, he's playing guitar and writing music.

IN THE KNOW

Full name: Austin Robert Butler
Birth date: August 17, 1991
Hometown: Anaheim, California
Zodiac sign: Leo
Fun fact: Austin collects guitars.

Looking lost in thought in New York's Central Park.

Didja know?

Austin went to public school until the seventh grade, but was homeschooled after that so he could fit his studies in with his work schedule.

BRADLEY STEVEN PERRY

Bradley began acting in movies when he was eight years old, and he made people laugh right from the start. That's probably what landed him the role of Gabe Duncan, the middle child trying to get used to having a younger sister, on *Good Luck Charlie*. In 2013, he landed a lead role on the Disney XD comedy *Mighty Med*, as a doctor in a hospital for superheroes. In real life, Bradley is kind of super himself: in spite of his busy shooting schedule, he manages to find time to help out the Make-A-Wish Foundation, Mattel Children's Hospital, and other good causes.

IN THE KNOW

Full name: **Bradley Steven Perry**
Birth date: **November 23, 1998**
Hometown: **Thousand Oaks, California**
Zodiac sign: **Sagittarius**

Casual! Bradley and Jason at the premiere of *Iron Man 3*.

At their first audition together for *Mighty Med,* Bradley and his co-star, Jake Short, were told, "We need you guys to be friends and bond"—even though they'd never met! It worked out well, though—they both play softball and get along great.

Didja know?

Bradley loves football, and even though he's from California, his favorite team is the New England Patriots. You might have seen him on commercials for *NBC Sunday Night Football* as "the Patriots Kid."

JASON DOLLEY

Movies, TV shows, Jason has done it all—even commercials for Duracell batteries. He rocked it as Newt Livingston III on the Disney Channel series *Cory in the House* and as the time-traveling high school hero Virgil Fox in the TV movie *Minutemen*. He received rave reviews for his role as Bridgit Mendler's goofy older brother on *Good Luck Charlie*. In an interview with the *Los Angeles Times* about the show, Jason said, "I like the realness of it. I like the more authentic tone."

IN THE KNOW

Full name: **Jason Scott Dolley**
Birth date: **July 5, 1991**
Hometown: **Simi Valley, California**
Zodiac sign: **Cancer**

Didja know?

Jason's first time on stage was at a school talent show, where he and his brother performed Abbott and Costello's funny "Who's on First?" routine.

Formal! Lookin' suave on the red carpet with his co-star at the Creative Emmy Awards.

5 SECONDS OF

5 Seconds of Summer is an Australian band that began when Luke Hemmings, Michael "Mikey" Clifford, and Calum Hood were classmates in school. They started posting covers of popular songs on YouTube in 2011. Later that year they found a drummer, Ashton Irwin, and 5 Seconds of Summer was ready to rock.

5SOS's debut single, "She Looks So Perfect," hit number one in thirty-nine countries, including the UK and Australia. Amazing! Their debut album kicked off Summer 2014. They called it *5 Seconds of Summer* because it represents who they are and where they're headed as a band.

SUMMER

The band, also known as 5SOS, released their first EP, *Unplugged*, in Summer 2012, and it reached number three on iTunes in Australia. They joined 1D on their "Take Me Home" tour in 2013, and again on their "Where We Are" stadium tour in 2014.

Didja know?

5SOS was voted Buzzworthy's "Fan-Favorite Breakthrough Band" in December 2013.

TYLER POSEY

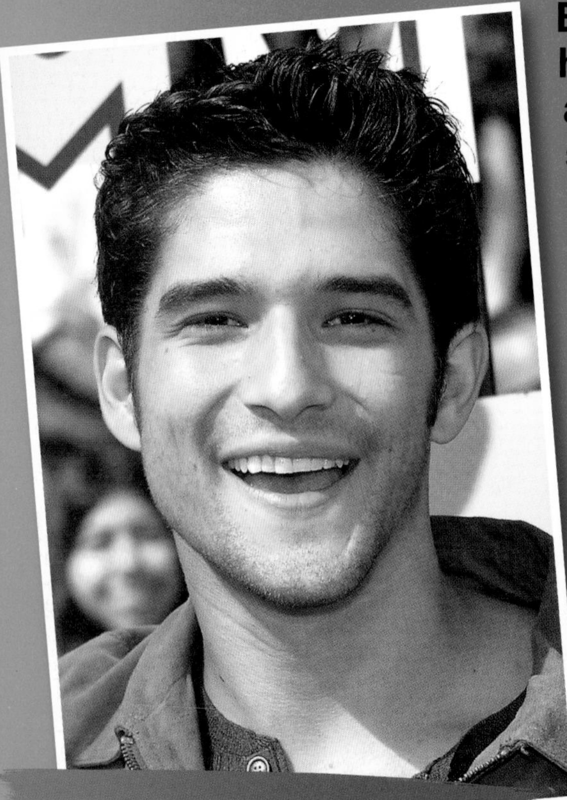

By the time he was a teenager, Tyler had already acted in several movies and popular TV series, including the shows *Doc* and *Smallville*. But it was in 2011, when he was twenty, that he got his big break in TV, landing the lead role in the MTV series *Teen Wolf*. His character, Scott McCall, struggles with the demands of maintaining his furry secret identity—but in real life, Tyler seems to have the juggling act all figured out. He has worked steadily in Hollywood for more than a decade and enjoys what he does. "I love being an entertainer and talking to people and making people feel good," he says. (*Collider.com*)

IN THE KNOW

Full name: **Tyler Garcia Posey**
Birth date: **October 18, 1991**
Hometown: **Valencia, California**
Zodiac sign: **Libra**

Enjoying a sweet treat at Universal Studios.

"I love action stuff, doing stunts, and playing the werewolf. It progresses more and more every time I do it—it gets a little more aggressive, which is really fun to play because there are no rules when it comes to playing a werewolf."
(EntertainmentWeekly.com)

AVAN JOGIA

Avan made a big splash as the down-to-earth Beck Oliver in the Nickelodeon TV show *Victorious*—and that's saying a lot, since he was surrounded by an all-star ensemble that included superstars Victoria Justice and Ariana Grande. The soundtracks from that musical show put the cast on the pop charts, too. Avan doesn't have to share the spotlight any more: he's starring in his own show on ABC Family, as the complex but charming Danny Desai in *Twisted*. But when asked about his dream role, Avan said that "it's not necessarily about being in the next big thing. If the character is interesting, they get under my skin and I can't shake them. That's when I know it's something I would like to do." (*Glamaholic.com*)

IN THE KNOW

Full name: Avan Tudor Jogia
Birth date: February 9, 1992
Hometown: Vancouver, British Columbia
Zodiac sign: Aquarius
Fun fact: Avan is a citizen of both Canada and Britain.

Flashing a winning smile at a *Victorious* fan.

TEEN WOLF

Tyler's character on *Teen Wolf* is no ordinary teenager. Scott McCall—a student bitten by a werewolf—has to figure out how to balance real life with being a werewolf. What does Tyler Posey think about his role on *Teen Wolf*? "I owe most of my acting chops to this show. I was a natural actor . . . but being on this show, I've learned so much. I've learned to be more subtle and more still, and that less is more," he told *Collider.com*.

Tyler says:

"I love being an entertainer and talking to people and making people feel good and opening up with people." (*Collider.com*)

HOW SWEET!

Tyler sends a special shout-out to his mom at the 2014 MTV Movie Awards.

TEEN WOLF CUTIES

Tyler Posey, Dylan O'Brien, twins Charlie and Max Carver, and Tyler Hoechlin goof off at Comic-Con.

Dylan's character, "Stiles" Stilinski, may not have supernatural powers like his best friend Scott, but he sure has cast a spell over fans with his goofy sense of humor that lightens up the show. Dylan is perfect for the role; when he was younger he loved posting funny short videos on YouTube.

Didja know?

Dylan is also a musician and plays the drums.

IN THE KNOW

Full name: Dylan O'Brien
Birth date: August 26, 1991
Hometown: New York, New York
Zodiac sign: Virgo

Tyler breakout role was playing Tom Hanks's son in the movie *Road to Perdition*. But he won our hearts in his recurring role as the talented young baseball player Martin Brewer on the popular family drama *7th Heaven*. A baseball player in college for real, Tyler likes the physical aspects of acting on *Teen Wolf*, especially doing fight scenes and stunt work when he has the opportunity. What's he like as a boyfriend? "It's all about reminding the other person how important and special she is to you," he told *Seventeen* magazine.

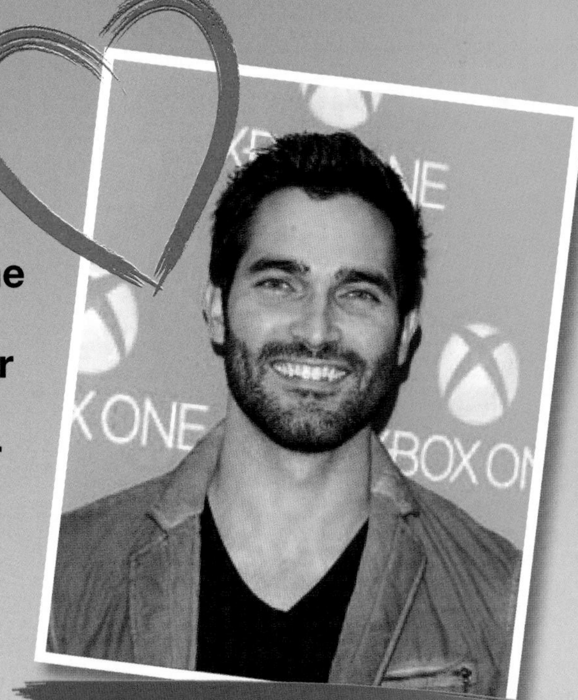

IN THE KNOW

Full name: Tyler Lee Hoechlin
Nickname: His baseball teammates called him "Hollywood."
Birth date: September 11, 1987
Hometown: Corona, California
Zodiac sign: Virgo

SHANE HARPER

Shane started dancing, acting, singing, and playing guitar and piano at the age of nine. But it was his dancing that first attracted the attention of Hollywood and landed him roles in *High School Musical*, *Dance Revolution*, and Nickelodeon's *Dance on Sunset*. It was all leading up to his role on *Good Luck Charlie*, playing Bridgit Mendler's on-again-off-again boyfriend, Spencer Walsh. But of course Shane wasn't about to let his musical talent go to waste: his first album came out in 2011 and includes a performance by the rapper Prophet and a duet with Bridgit. His song "Let's Take the World Tonight" can be heard in the movie *Blue Lagoon: The Awakening.*

IN THE KNOW

Full name: **Shane Steven Harper**
Birth date: **February 14, 1993**
Hometown: **San Diego, California**
Zodiac sign: **Aquarius**
Fun fact: **The deluxe version of Shane's first album was released on his birthday in 2012.**

Shane crooning for Radio Disney at the Magnificent Mile Lights festival in Chicago.

Didja know?

Shane earned his black belt in karate at the age of twelve.

GREGG SULKIN

Growing up in London, soccer was Gregg's big thing—he'd never even thought about acting until an injury kept him out of the game for a year and he had to find something else to do with his energy. "I fell in love with [acting] when I realized how amazing, difficult, and interesting it is," he told *Teen Vogue.* After landing parts in TV shows and movies in England, Gregg grabbed the lead—and girls' hearts—in the Disney series *As the Bell Rings*. And once he put on his werewolf costume for *Wizards of Waverly Place* and shared his first on-screen kiss with Selena Gomez, there was no going back to soccer!

Dimple alert!

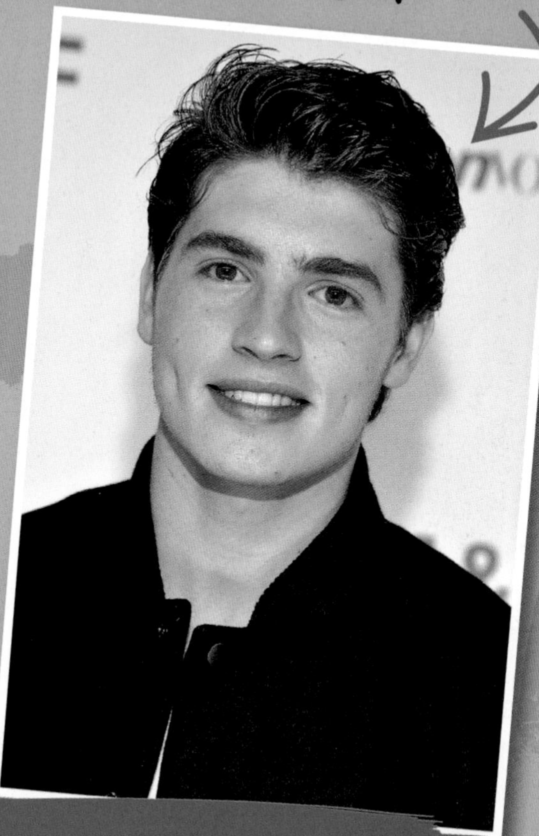

IN THE KNOW

Full name: **Gregg Sulkin**
Birth date: **May 29, 1992**
Hometown: **London, England**
Zodiac sign: **Taurus**

Rocking the MTV red carpet.

What is the way to Gregg's heart? *"I think if a girl gets along with my family that's really important. If she can hang out with my guy friends and hang out with my family."* (Missoandfriends.com)

BILLY UNGER

By the time Billy was ten years old, he knew he wanted to be an actor. A year later, his family moved from Florida to Los Angeles, and it wasn't long before he was making that dream come true. Since 2007, he's appeared in dozens of movies and TV shows—and is currently driving fans wild as the superhuman Chase Davenport on the Disney XD comedy *Lab Rats*. Chase isn't just strong, he's also brainy, which is one of the reasons Billy loves playing him. "When I open a script I seem to always walk away with a couple of new words to add to my vocab," he told *KellyCrossman.com*.

IN THE KNOW

Full name: William Brent Unger
Nickname: Billy
Birth date: October 15, 1995
Hometown: Palm Beach County, Florida
Zodiac sign: Libra

Billy signing a poster for a fan at the 2013 D23 Expo.

TRY TO KEEP UP!

Besides acting, Billy's favorite activities are extreme martial arts, motocross, surfing, skateboarding, hip-hop dancing, singing, and playing guitar. He plays guitar and sings in a band called the Painkillers.

NICHOLAS HOULT

IN THE KNOW

Full name: Nicholas Caradoc Hoult
Birth date: December 7, 1989
Hometown: Wokingham, Berkshire, England
Zodiac sign: Sagittarius
Fun fact: He danced in English National Ballet productions of *Swan Lake* and *The Nutcracker.*

What is so special about Nicholas? Start with his dreamy British accent and baby-blue eyes. . . and add the fact that he's figured out how to play it cool and super-intense at the same time. His early roles were in television—until he stole the spotlight from Hugh Grant in the 2002 movie *About a Boy*. (Impressive, since he was only twelve at the time!) Other movie roles followed, including Beast in *X-Men: First Class* and *X-Men: Days of Future Past*. It might be a little hard to see him under all that makeup, but Nicholas's star power definitely shines through.

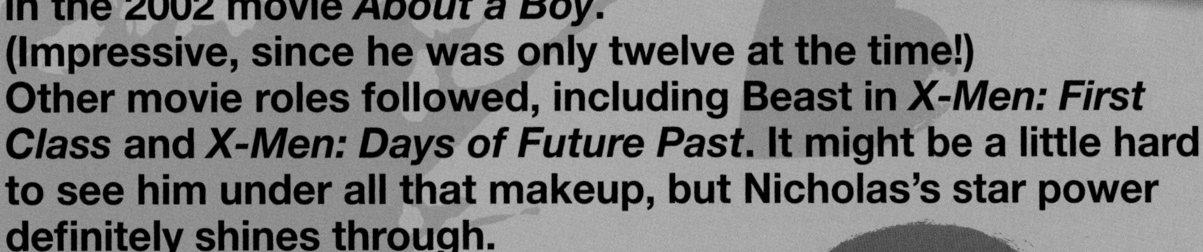

WOW!
Nicholas has won four Teen Choice Awards—one of them for "Choice Movie Chemistry."

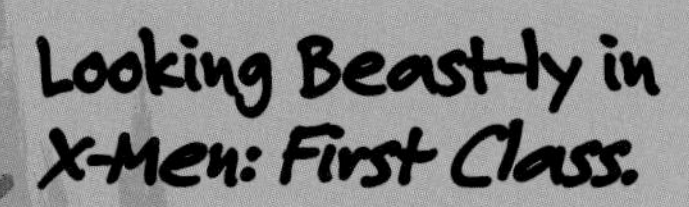
Looking Beast-ly in *X-Men: First Class.*

CUTE AND CUDDLY

Everyone loves a furry friend, and these guys are no exception.

1D gets an armful of puppies during a radio show appearance.

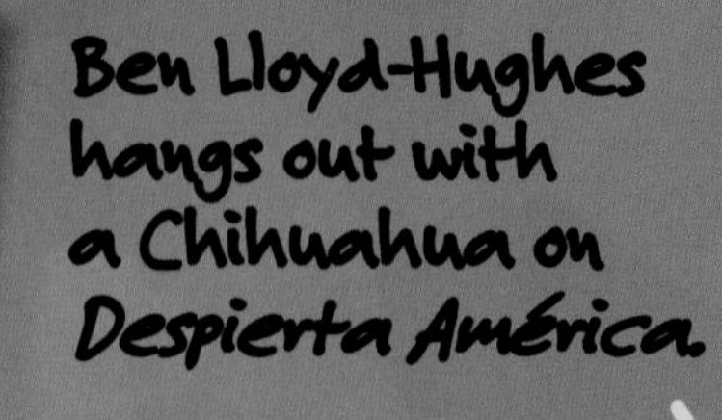

Ben Lloyd-Hughes hangs out with a Chihuahua on *Despierta América*.

Jacob Artist gets a kiss from Uggie, the doggie actor who won hearts in *The Artist*.

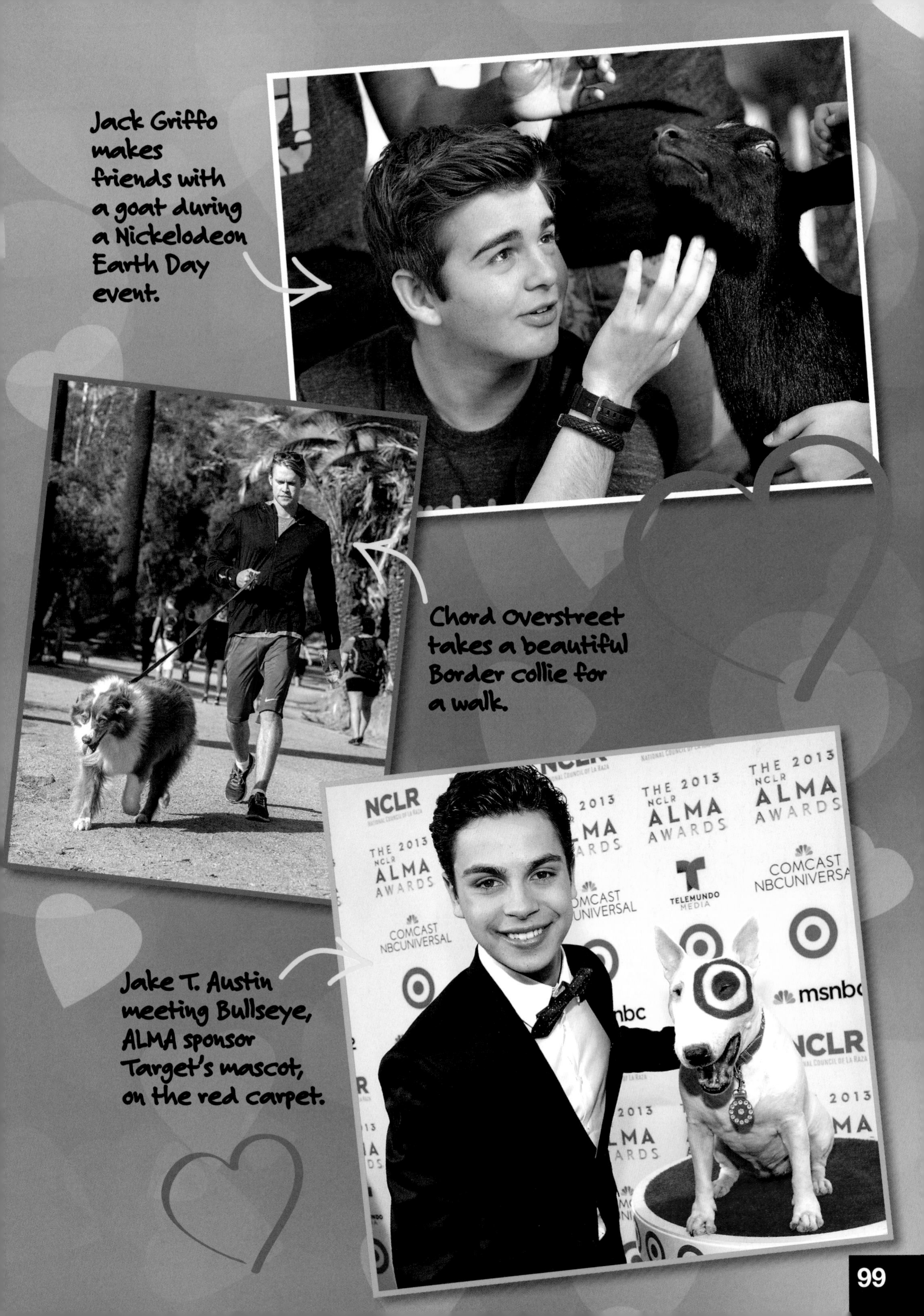

Jack Griffo makes friends with a goat during a Nickelodeon Earth Day event.

Chord Overstreet takes a beautiful Border collie for a walk.

Jake T. Austin meeting Bullseye, ALMA sponsor Target's mascot, on the red carpet.

PRETTY LITTLE LIARS

No television show has quite as many tricks up its sleeve as *Pretty Little Liars*, and while it may be noted for its plot twists, it also has some spotlight-stealing leading men.

Ian seemed sympathetic and trustworthy in his breakout role as teacher Ezra Fitz, but things change quickly on *Pretty Little Liars*. Even Ian doesn't know what's going to happen next. "I'm only a few steps ahead of the audience," he told *Zap2it.com*. Ian started developing his acting chops early, making up stories to get out of trouble when he was a kid. "I would make up a lie and I would just really believe in it," he told *Interview*. Now he has to keep secrets in his role on the show, and when talking about the show—no spoilers from Ian!

IN THE KNOW

Full name: **Ian Harding**
Birth date: **September 13, 1986**
Hometown: **North Bethesda, Maryland**
Zodiac sign: **Virgo**

xoxo

Supporting the cause—keeping students in school and on track to graduate—at the 2014 City Year Los Angeles "Spring Break" Fundraiser.

Keegan grew up around acting: his dad, Phillip Richard Allen, had a successful career in movies, on television, and on stage. Growing up around show business, Keegan at first thought he'd like to work behind the camera. But a few acting opportunities—including a guest spot on Nickelodeon's *Big Time Rush*—changed his path. Keegan originally auditioned for the part of Wren on *Pretty Little Liars*, but was chosen to play Spencer's love interest, Toby Cavanaugh, instead. Nominated for a Teen Choice Award as Summer TV Star in 2011, Keegan won in 2013.

IN THE KNOW

Full name: Keegan Phillip Allen
Birth date: July 22, 1989
Hometown: Los Angeles, California
Zodiac sign: Cancer

Onstage with Randy Jackson and Steven Tyler at 2014's Race to Erase MS in Los Angeles.

Tyler got his start in acting on the Nickelodeon series *Unfabulous* in 2002, but *Pretty Little Liars* has given him a chance to shine. As Hanna's love interest and resident bad boy Caleb Rivers, Tyler gives a riveting performance.

Tyler is also a talented musician, and he recorded a soundtrack song for the TV show *The Secret Life of the American Teenager*.

IN THE KNOW

Full name: Tyler Jordon Blackburn
Nickname: Ty
Birth date: October 12, 1986
Hometown: Burbank, California
Zodiac sign: Libra

HOT RODS

The stars know a cool guy needs a cool ride.

On a motorcycle or in a car, BTR's James Maslow hits the road in style.

Nicholas Hoult looking sleek at the premiere of the 380-horsepower Jaguar F-TYPE Coupe.

Josh Hutcherson on his Deus EX Machina cycle cruisin' LA.

Spencer Boldman trying out a superpowered ride at the premiere of *The Avengers*.

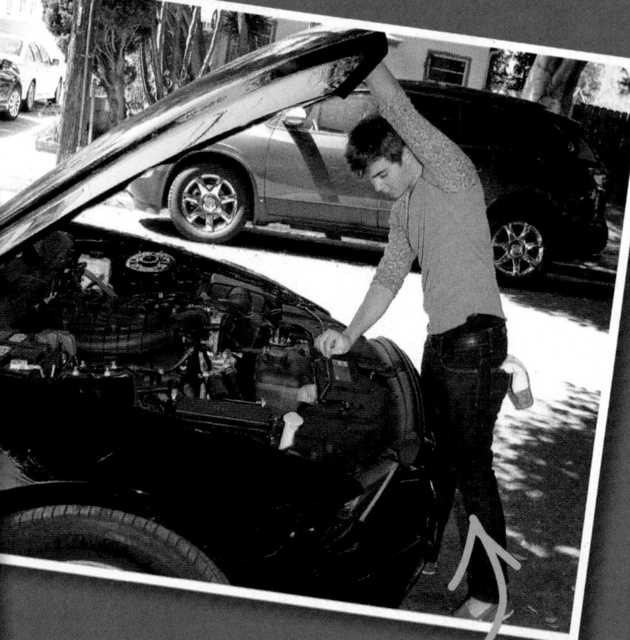

Jack Griffo checking under the hood of his sports car. Hope he can fix it!

Nice ride, Leo Howard!

Sweet wheels, Cody Simpson!

DARREN CRISS

Darren got his start starring as Harry Potter in the hit YouTube parody *A Very Potter Musical*, sang his way onto the Broadway stage in *How to Succeed in Business Without Really Trying*, and is pitch-perfect as Blaine Anderson on the TV show *Glee*. It is the ideal role for a guy who can do it all: act, sing, and dance. He also plays the guitar, piano, harmonica, and drums.

IN THE KNOW

Full name: **Darren Criss**
Nickname: **Dare**
Birth date: **February 5, 1987**
Hometown: **San Francisco, California**
Zodiac sign: **Aquarius**

Darren shooting a scene for *Glee* in NYC.

Is Darren a Directioner? Love him even more!

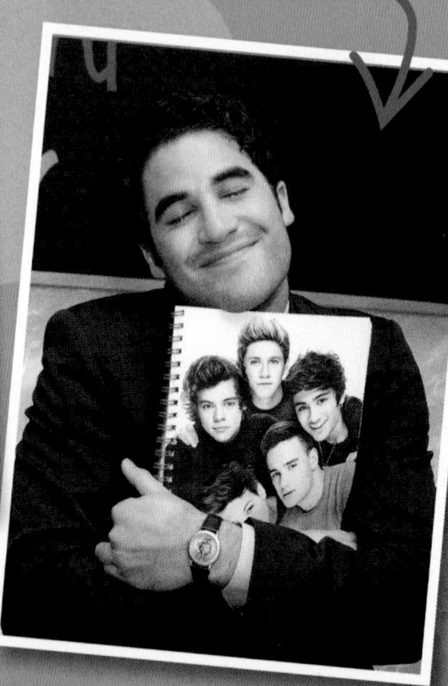

CHORD OVERSTREET

Does Chord's name sound musical? He comes from a creative family. Chord's father is a country music singer-songwriter, and his mother is a makeup artist. He has four sisters and an older brother who is a professional musician. He grew up on a farm outside Nashville.

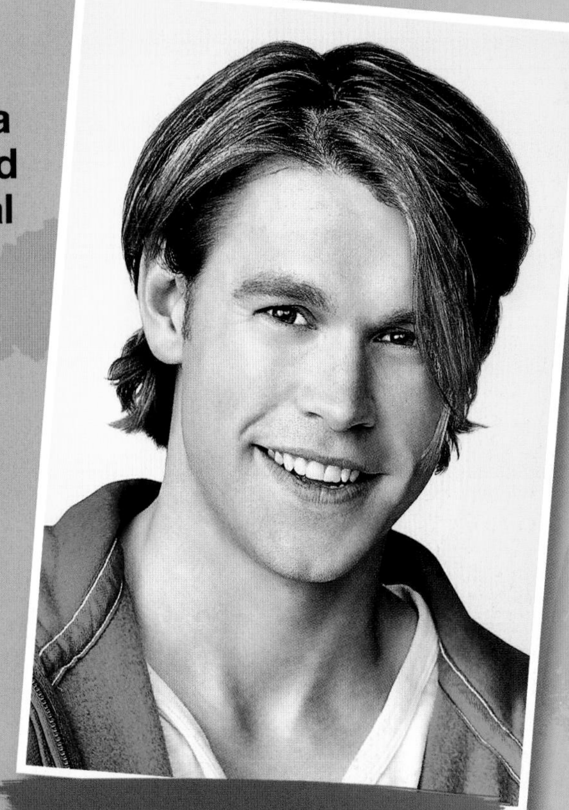

Chord stars as Sam Evans, the cutie-pie jock, on *Glee*. Sam is a great athlete and all-around good guy who is always looking out for his friends. In real life, that describes Chord perfectly. He is an amazing musician—not only can he sing a great rock anthem, he also plays the mandolin, flute, drums, and guitar.

IN THE KNOW

Full name: **Chord Overstreet**
Birth date: **February 17, 1989**
Hometown: **Nashville, Tennessee**
Zodiac sign: **Aquarius**
Loves to: **Do impersonations**

With co-star Darren Criss in a scene from *Glee*.

EMBLEM3

In 2013, brothers Wesley and Keaton Stromberg, along with their friend Drew Chadwick, signed a record deal based on their incredible performances on *The X Factor USA* (they finished fourth). Soon afterward they became the opening act for Selena Gomez on her "Star Dance Tour." They announced their own headlining tour, "#bandlife," in 2014.

FACE TIME

KEATON STROMBERG

DREW CHADWICK

WESLEY STROMBERG

Didja know?

Emblem3 won "Breakout Group" at the Teen Choice Awards in 2013.

Drew catches air on stage.

When asked to describe Emblem3's album *Nothing to Lose,* Wesley told *OK!* magazine, "It's a very summery, light vibe that's ready to put you in a good mood anytime, anywhere."

TRAVELING GUYS

Being an actor or a musician means a lot of jet-setting. Check out where your favorite stars have been spotted lately.

Looks like Texan Austin Mahone forgot to bring a coat with him to chilly NYC.

Ed Sheeran surrounded by fans at a train station in Paris.

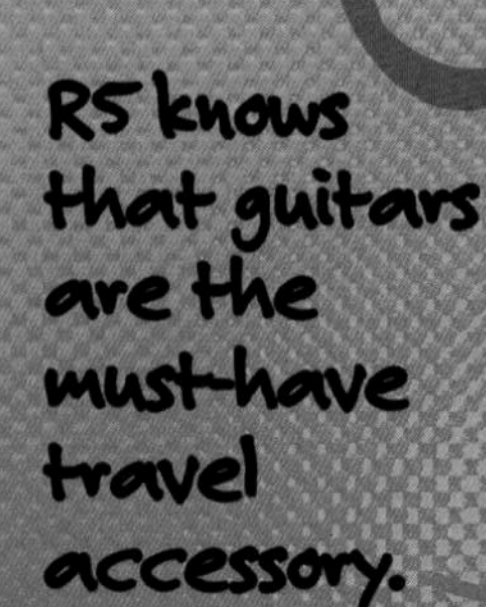

R5 knows that guitars are the must-have travel accessory.

1D arrives dressed for the occasion in Tokyo.

Robert Pattinson arrives in Melbourne, Australia, with his trusty guitar in hand.

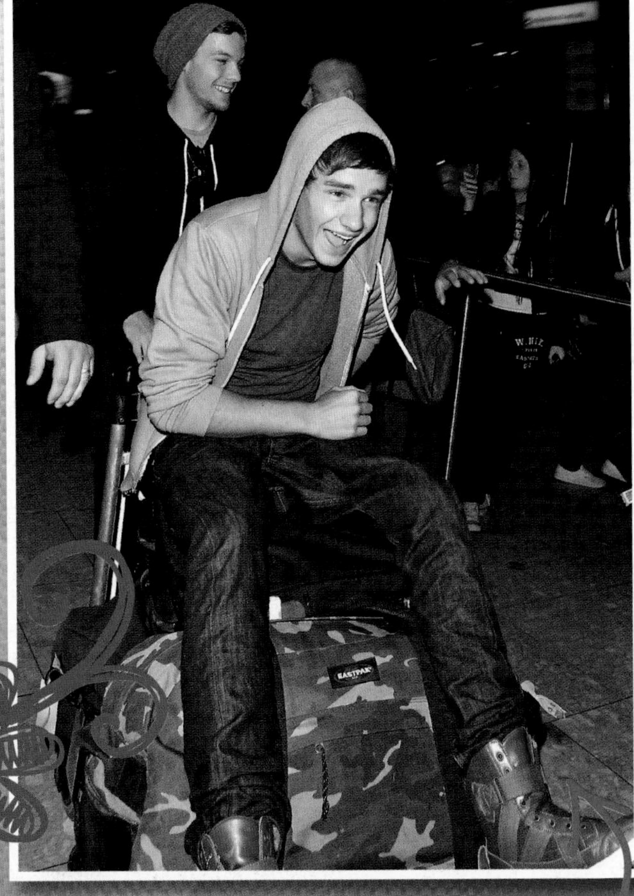

Liam Payne hitches a ride on Louis Tomlinson's suitcases in London.

GOOD DEEDS

Whether raising awareness and money for charities or donating their time, our favorite stars know that fame and success mean nothing if you don't give back to the causes that matter most.

Cody Simpson encouraged his fans to make stuffed animals for the US Marine Toys for Tots Foundation "Stuffed with Hugs" Build-a-Bear Workshop event.

Keegan Allen, Tyler Blackburn, and actress Aimee Teegarden hang with an adorable sea turtle plushie to raise awareness for ocean life conservation at the Oceana Beach House event.

One Direction teamed up with Office Depot to raise $1 million for anti-bullying education in schools across America. 1D + OD Together Against Bullying—mission accomplished!

Emblem3 performed at the "Rock the Red Kettle" concert to support the Salvation Army.

The Wanted supported the United States Tennis Association's charity, which provides tennis and educational support programs for at-risk students and people with disabilities, at Arthur Ashe Kids' Day at the US Open in New York.

Jack Griffo promotes earth-friendly living at the 2014 Nickelodeon "Get Dirty!" Earth Day event at the Los Angeles Zoo.

PHOTO CREDITS:1:©Aleksander Erin/Shutterstock.**2-3:**©Alyasandra/Dreamstime.**2:**top left:©Mat Hayward/Getty Images;top right:©Kevin Winter/Billboard Awards 2014/Getty Images;bottom left:©Jeff Kravitz/FilmMagic;bottom middle:©Dan MacMedan/WireImage;bottom right:©Jo Hale/Redferns/Getty Images.**3:**top:©Kevin Mazur/WireImage;bottom:©Matt Petit/Disney ABC Television Group.**4-5:**©Cristian Dina/Dreamstime.**6-7:**©Jamie McCarthy/Getty Images.**7:**middle:©Dave J Hogan/Getty Images;all other images:©David M.Benett/Getty Images.**8-9:**©Cristian Dina/Dreamstime.**8:**top:©Mike Marsland/WireImage;middle:©Splash/HardlyEverWornIt/Splash News/Corbis;bottom:©James Whatling/Splash News/Corbis.**9:**top left:©Rabbani and Solimene Photography/WireImage;top right:©Mike Marsland/WireImage;bottom:©Jamie McCarthy/Getty Images.**10-11:**©Cristian Dina/Dreamstime.**10:**top:©Jason Merritt/Getty Images;bottom:©Piko Press/Splash News/Corbis.**11:**top:©Mike Marsland/WireImage;bottom:©Grupo13/LatinContent/Getty Images.**12-13:**©Cristian Dina/Dreamstime.**12:**top:©Mirrorpix/Splash News/Corbis;middle:©Keith Tsuji/Getty Images;bottom:©Jeff Kravitz/FilmMagic.**13:**top:©Fred Duval/FilmMagic;bottom:©Peter Kramer/NBC/NBC NewsWire/Getty Images.**14-15:**©Cristian Dina/Dreamstime.**14:**top:©David Livingston/Getty Images;bottom:©Gilbert Carrasquillo/Getty Images.**15:**top:©Mark Davis/Getty Images;bottom:©Alberto Rodriguez/KCA2014/Getty Images.**16-17:**©Chelsea Lauren/Getty Images.**17:**top:©David Livingston/Getty Images;top middle:©Ilya S.Savenok/Getty Images;middle:©Cindy Ord/Getty Images;last two:©Ilya S.Savenok/Getty Images.**18-19:**©Cristian Dina/Dreamstime.**18:**top:©Tommaso Boddi/WireImage;bottom:©Rick Diamond/WireImage.**19:**top:©Tommaso Boddi/WireImage;bottom:©Jo Hale/Redferns/Getty Images.**20-21:**©Cristian Dina/Dreamstime.**20:**top:©Brent Perniac/AdMedia/Corbis;bottom:©Paul A.Hebert/Invision/AP.**21:**top:©Don Arnold/WireImage;bottom:©DFL/Splash/Corbis.**22-23:**©Nina Susik/Shutterstock.**22:**left:©Jonathan Leibson/Getty Images for PMC;right:©Jim McIsaac/Getty Images.**23:**top:©Kevin Mazur/FOX/WireImage;middle:©Rommel Demano/FilmMagic;bottom:©Jeff Kravitz/FilmMagic.**24-25:**©Cristian Dina/Dreamstime.**24:**top:©Steve Granitz/WireImage;bottom:©Rich Polk/Getty Images for Variety.**25:**top:©FOX/Getty Images;bottom:©Tyler Golden/Oxygen Media/NBCU Photo Bank/Getty Images.**26:**top:©Mike Marsland/WireImage;bottom:©Lloyd Bishop/NBC/NBCU Photo Bank/Getty Images.**27:**top:©Gary Gershoff/WireImage;middle:©Jeff Kravitz/FilmMagic;middle bottom:©Joshua Blanchard/Getty Images;bottom:©Cindy Ord/Getty Images.**28:**left:©Larry Busacca/VF14/Getty Images for Vanity Fair;right:©Jim Spellman/WireImage.**29:**top left:©Michel Dufour/WireImage;top right:©Anthony Harvey/FilmMagic;bottom:©Gregg DeGuire/WireImage.**30-31:**©Cristian Dina/Dreamstime.**30:**top:©Amanda Edwards/WireImage;middle:©Paul Hiffmeyer/Disney Parks/Getty Images;bottom:©Gregg DeGuire/WireImage.**31:**top:©Angela Weiss/Getty Images;bottom:©Rick Diamond/Getty Images for BET's Rip The Runway.**32-33:**©Cristian Dina/Dreamstime.**32:**top:©Omar Vega/Invision for OP/AP Images;bottom:©MCCFL/Splash News/Corbis.**33:**top:©Alexander Tamargo/Getty Images;bottom left:©Splash News/Corbis;bottom right:©Ben Horton/WireImage.**34:**top:©Carlos Alvarez/Getty Images;bottom:©Splash News/Corbis.**35:**top:©Vera Anderson/WireImage;middle:©Jon Kopaloff/FilmMagic;bottom:©donatas1205/Shutterstock.**36-37:**©Cristian Dina/Dreamstime.**36:**top:©Jason LaVeris/FilmMagic;bottom:©Frederick M.Brown/Getty Images.**37:**top:©Bob King/Corbis;bottom:©Joel Ryan/Invision/AP.**38-39:**©Ollie Millington/Redferns/Getty Images.**38:**top two:©Tim P.Whitby/Getty Images;middle bottom:©Eamonn McCormack/WireImage;bottom:©Tim P.Whitby/Getty Images.**40-41:**©Melpomenem/Dreamstime.**40:**left:©Jason LaVeris/FilmMagic;top right:©Gregg DeGuire/WireImage;bottom right:©Jon Kopaloff/FilmMagic.**41:**top:©Michael Buckner/Getty Images;middle:©Fred Duval/FilmMagic;bottom:©David M.Benett/Getty Images.**42-43:**©Scott Legato/Getty Images.**43:**top:©Daniel Zuchnik/Getty Images;middle:©Robin Marchant/Getty Images;bottom three:©Daniel Zuchnik/Getty Images.**44-45:**©Cristian Dina/Dreamstime.**44:**top left:©Amanda Edwards/WireImage;top right:©Jason Merritt/Getty Images;bottom left:©Dave M.Benett/Getty Images;bottom right:©Mike Pont/FilmMagic.**45:**top left:©Jeffrey Mayer/WireImage;top right:©Kevin Mazur/WireImage;bottom left:©Larry Busacca/Getty Images for MTV;bottom right:©Kevin Mazur/WireImage for MTV.**46-47:**©Phasin/Dreamstime.**46:**top:©Theo Wargo/WireImage;bottom:©Frederick M.Brown/Getty Images.**47:**top:©Victor Chavez/WireImage;middle:©Ethan Miller/Getty Images;bottom:©Kevin Mazur/WireImage.**48-49:**©Cristian Dina/Dreamstime.**48:**top:©Jason Merritt/Getty Images Entertainment;bottom left:©Ben Buchanan/Wild Life Sydney Zoo/Getty Images;bottom right:©Araya Diaz/Getty Images for Queen Mary's Chill.**49:**top:©Jason Kempin/WireImage;bottom:©Gabriel Olsen/FilmMagic.**50-51:**background:©Cristian Dina/Dreamstime;all other images:©Seth Poppel/Yearbook Library.**52:**top:©Jeff Kravitz/FilmMagic;bottom:©Loic Venance/AFP/Getty Images.**53:**top left:©Christopher Polk/WireImage;top right:©AP Photo/Donald Traill;bottom left:©Ethan Miller/WireImage;bottom right:©Paul Archuleta/FilmMagic.**54-55:**©Aleksander Erin/Shutterstock.**54:**top left:©Paul Hiffmeyer/Disney Parks/Getty Images;top right:©Amanda Edwards/WireImage;bottom left:©Lester Cohen/WireImage;bottom right:©Paul Morigi/WireImage.**55:**top left:©Shirlaine Forrest/WireImage;top right:©Raymond Hall/GC Images;bottom left:©Dana Edelson/NBC/NBCU Photo Bank/Getty Images;bottom right:©Jeff Kravitz/FilmMagic.**56-57:**©Cristian Dina/Dreamstime.**56:**top:©Frederick M.Brown/Getty Images;bottom:©Christopher Polk/WireImage.**57:**top:©Ari Perilstein/Getty Images for Variety;bottom:©Kevin Winter/Getty Images for NCLR.**58-59:**©Cristian Dina/Dreamstime.**58:**top:©Theo Wargo/Getty Images;bottom:©Joey Foley/Getty Images.**59:**top left:©Michael Stewart/Getty Images for Oakley;top right:©Jesal Parshotam/Splash News/Corbis;bottom two:©Splash News/Corbis.**60-61:**©Cristian Dina/Dreamstime.**60:**©Christopher Polk/Getty Images for NARAS.**61:**top:©Gareth Cattermole/TAS/Getty Images for TAS;bottom two:©Kevin Mazur/WireImage.**62-63:**©Victor Chavez/WireImage.**63:**top:©Jason Merritt/Getty Images;top middle:©Frazer Harrison/Getty Images;bottom middle:©David Livingston/Getty Images;bottom:©Chelsea Lauren/WireImage.**64-65:**©Alyasandra/Dreamstime.**64:**top:©Christopher Polk/WireImage;middle:©Mike Pont/FilmMagic;bottom:©Shirlaine Forrest/WireImage.**65:**top:©Andy Kropa/Getty Images;middle:©Richard S/Splash News/Corbis;bottom:©Scott Legato/Getty Images.**66-67:**©Cristian Dina/Dreamstime.**66:**top:©Mike Windle/WireImage;bottom:©Charley Gallay/Getty Images for Nickelodeon.**67:**top:©David Livingston/Getty Images;bottom:©AP Photo/Relativity Media/Philippe Antonello.**68-69:**©Cristian Dina/Dreamstime.**68:**top:©Kevin Mazur/WireImage;bottom two:©Splash News/Corbis.**69:**top:©Gustavo Caballero/Getty Images;middle:©Pierre Suu/Getty Images;bottom:©Michael Becker/FOX/Getty Images.**70-71:**©mythja/Shutterstock.**70:**1.©Daniel Zuchnik/Getty Images;2.©Gilbert Carrasquillo/FilmMagic;3.©Jerod Harris/WireImage.**71:**4.©JB Lacroix/WireImage;5.©Chelsea Lauren/WireImage;6.©RV/Bauer-Griffin/GC Images;7.©Jeffery Duran/Celebrity Monitor/Splash News/Corbis;8.©Blayze/Splash News/Corbis.**72-73:**©Leigh Prather/Shutterstock.**72:**top:©Dave J Hogan/Getty Images;bottom:©Jeff Kravitz/FilmMagic.**73:**top:©Theo Wargo/WireImage;middle:©Kevin Mazur/WireImage;bottom:©Steve Granitz/WireImage.**74-75:**©Cristian Dina/Dreamstime.**74:**top:©Paul Archuleta/WireImage;bottom:©Kevan Brooks/AdMedia/Corbis.**75:**top:©Jon Kopaloff/FilmMagic;bottom:©FOX/Getty Images.**76-77:**©Cristian Dina/Dreamstime.**76:**top:©Valerie Macon/Getty Images;bottom:©Kevin Winter/Getty Images for Race to Erase MS.**77:**top:©Ben A.Pruchnie/Getty Images for Nickelodeon;bottom:©Timothy Hiatt/Getty Images for Radio.**78-79:**©Cristian Dina/Dreamstime.**78:**top:©Frederick M.Brown/Getty Images;bottom:©Maryland School for the Deaf.**79:**top:©Valerie Macon/Getty Images;bottom:©Michael Tran/FilmMagic.**80-81:**©Cristian Dina/Dreamstime.**80:**top left:©Frazer Harrison/Getty Images;top right:©FOX/Getty Images;bottom:©Frank Trapper/Corbis.**81:**top left:©Aaron Davidson/Getty Images;top right:©Gregg DeGuire/WireImage;middle:©Cindy Ord/Getty Images;bottom:©LAN/Corbis.**82-83:**©Cristian Dina/Dreamstime.**82:**top:©terra.com.pe/Splash News/Corbis;bottom left:©All Access Photo/Splash News/Corbis;bottom right:©Wylde/Splash News/Corbis.**83:**top left:©GoldenEye/London Entertainment/Splash News/Corbis;top right:©London Ent/Splash News/Corbis;bottom left:©EM43/Splash News/Corbis;bottom right:©Marcus/Zodiac/Splash News/Corbis.**84-85:**©Cristian Dina/Dreamstime.**84:**top:©David Livingston/Getty Images;bottom:©Olivier Douliery-Pool/Getty Images.**85:**top:©Charles Norfleet/FilmMagic;bottom:©Alo Ceballos/FilmMagic.**86-87:**©Cristian Dina/Dreamstime.**86:**top:©Christopher Polk/WireImage;bottom:©Jeffrey Mayer/WireImage.**87:**top:©Steve Granitz/WireImage;bottom:©Tommaso Boddi/WireImage.**88-89:**©David Wolff-Patrick/Redferns/Getty Images.**89:**top:©Scott Weiner/Retna Ltd./Corbis;top middle:©Anthony Harvey/Getty Images;bottom middle:©Splash News/Corbis;bottom:©Anthony Harvey/Getty Images.**90-91:**©Cristian Dina/Dreamstime.**90:**top:©Michael Buckner/Getty Images;bottom:©Jeff Kravitz/FilmMagic.**91:**top:©Jon Kopaloff/FilmMagic;©Brendan Hoffman/Getty Images for Nickelodeon.**92:**top:©Jon Kopaloff/FilmMagic;middle:©Christopher Polk/Getty Images for MTV;bottom:©Chelsea Lauren/WireImage.**93:**top:©Jon Kopaloff/FilmMagic;bottom:©Paul Archuleta/FilmMagic.**94-95:**©Cristian Dina/Dreamstime.**94:**top:©All Access Photo/Splash News/Corbis;bottom:©Timothy Hiatt/Getty Images.**95:**top:©John M.Heller/Getty Images;bottom:©Jason Merritt/Getty Images for MTV.**96-97:**©Cristian Dina/Dreamstime.**96:**top:©Frazer Harrison/Getty Images;bottom:©Matt Petit/D23 Expo/Getty Images.**97:**top:©Jim Spellman/WireImage;bottom:©Murray Close/Getty Images.**98-99:**©Cristian Dina/Dreamstime.**98:**top:©Bill McCay/WireImage;bottom left:©Chelsea Lauren/WireImage;bottom right:©Alexander Tamargo/Getty Images.**99:**top:©Charley Gallay/Getty Images for Nickelodeon;middle:©Christopher Polk/WireImage;bottom:©John Sciulli/Getty Images for Target.**100:**top:©Gregg DeGuire/Getty Images;bottom:©Michael Bezjian/Getty Images for City Year Los Angeles;**101:**top:©Alberto E.Rodriguez/Getty Images for Race to Erase MS;middle:©Michael Buckner/Getty Images for Race to Erase MS;bottom:©Michael Buckner/Getty Images.**102-103:**©Nina Susik/Shutterstock.**102:**top:©JMA/Star Max/GC Images;middle:©Cathy Gibson/Splash News/Corbis;bottom left:©Xavier Collin/Celebrity Monitor/Splash News/Corbis;bottom right:©JLM/Splash News/Corbis.**103:**top left:©Lester Cohen/WireImage;top right:©Jen Lowery/Splash News/Corbis;bottom left:©Alexandra Wyman/Invision for Talent Resources/AP Images;bottom right:©Lisa Rose/ZUMA Press/Corbis.**104-105:**©Cristian Dina/Dreamstime.**104:**top:©Walter McBride/WireImage;bottom left:©Raymond Hall/GC Images;bottom right:©Mark Sullivan/WireImage.**105:**both images:©FOX/Getty Images.**106-107:**Scott Legato/Getty Images.**106:**top:©Kevin Kane/WireImage;middle:©David Livingston/Getty Images;bottom:©Ilen Berezovsky/WireImage.**107:**Joey Foley/Getty Images.**108-109:**©Cristian Dina/Dreamstime.**108:**top left:©247PapsTV/Splash News/Corbis;top right:©Marc Piasecki/GC Images;bottom:©Jun Sato/WireImage.**109:**top:©Jun Sato/WireImage;bottom two:©Splash News/Corbis.**110-111:**©Alyasandra/Dreamstime.**110:**top left:©Slaven Vlasic/Getty Images;top right:©David Livingston/Getty Images;bottom:©Jeff Kravitz/FilmMagic.**111:**top left:©Chelsea Lauren/WireImage;top right:©Uri Schanker/Getty Images;bottom left:©Charley Gallay/Getty Images for Nickelodeon.**112:**©Aleksander Erin/Shutterstock.
Note: All heart graphics ©iktash/Shutterstock, all flower graphics ©Kytalpa/Dreamstime.